*The Art of Sauces & Condiments: Craftir*
Jasper B. Monroe

# Introduction

Welcome to the world of condiments and sauces—a place where a humble spoonful can transform a meal from ordinary to unforgettable. I'm Jasper B. Monroe, and I've spent a lifetime chasing the perfect blend of tang, spice, and soul. To me, these aren't just toppings or afterthoughts; they're the heartbeat of every dish, the secret weapon that makes food sing. This book is my love letter to the craft of making them from scratch, and I'm thrilled to share it with you.

My obsession started in a small Louisiana kitchen, where the air buzzed with the hum of cicadas and the sizzle of my grandmother Eula's roux. She was a wizard with a spoon, turning vinegar, peppers, and a pinch of magic into jars of pickled relish and hot sauce that could wake up any plate. "A meal's only as good as what you put on it, cher," she'd say, and at eight years old, I took that to heart. She handed me a spoon one sticky summer day and let me tweak her barbecue sauce—my first taste of creating something that made people smile. From then on, I was hooked.

That spark followed me through life. In the Navy, I traded bland chow-line grub for scribbled recipes from every port—fiery harissa from Tunisia, a sticky soy glaze from Tokyo, a smoky chipotle sauce from Mexico. I'd tinker with them in my bunk by lantern light, dreaming of the day I could bottle those flavors myself. When I landed in Austin, Texas, my backyard became a laboratory. Friends would swing by, leaving with jars of mustard or fermented garlic honey, and I'd grin as they begged for more. But it was a rainy afternoon, when I whipped up a chimichurri for a dull steak and saw my wife's eyes light up, that I knew: this was my calling. Why settle for store-bought when you can make it better?

Homemade condiments and sauces are about more than flavor—they're about taking charge of what you eat. You control the heat, the sweetness, the zing. You decide if that ketchup has a kick or that mayo gets a truffle twist. There's a thrill in watching simple ingredients—tomatoes, herbs, a splash of vinegar—turn into something extraordinary. Plus, it's personal. Every jar carries a story, a memory, a little piece of where I've been, from Grandma Eula's kitchen to a bustling street market halfway across the world.

In these pages, you'll find recipes for the classics—ketchup, mayo, mustard—alongside global gems like chimichurri and gochujang, and a few surprises I've dreamed up along the way. I'll walk you through the essentials: the tools (nothing fancy needed), the pantry staples (you've probably got half already), and tips for storing your creations so they last. Whether you're dipping, drizzling, or slathering, my goal is to help you craft flavors that make every bite your own.

So grab a spoon, a jar, and a little curiosity. Let's make something delicious together—because a great meal starts with what you put on it.

# Chapter 1: The Classics

There's something sacred about the condiments we grow up with—those jars and bottles that sit on every table, waiting to make a burger sing or a fry dance. For me, it all circles back to ketchup. I'll never forget the summer I turned ten, standing in Grandma Eula's kitchen as she decided it was time I learned her recipe. She'd been tweaking it since before I was born, a sweet-tangy mix that clung to fried catfish like a glove. The kitchen smelled of simmering tomatoes and vinegar, and she handed me a wooden spoon, saying, "Stir it slow, Jasper—good things take time." I burned my tongue sneaking a taste before it cooled, but that first lick of her ketchup ruined me for the store-bought stuff forever. It's where this chapter begins—because the classics aren't just recipes; they're memories we can remake, one batch at a time. Here are ten to get you started.

# 1. Traditional Tomato Ketchup

**Yield:** About 2 cups (480 ml)

**Prep Time:** 15 minutes

**Cook Time:** 1 hour

**Ingredients:**

- 2 lbs (900 g) ripe tomatoes, chopped
- 1 cup (240 ml) white vinegar
- ½ cup (100 g) granulated sugar
- 1 small onion (about 4 oz / 113 g), finely chopped
- 1 tsp (5 g) salt
- ½ tsp (2 g) ground black pepper
- ¼ tsp (1 g) ground cloves
- ¼ tsp (1 g) ground allspice

**Instructions:**

1. Start by prepping your ingredients: roughly chop the tomatoes into bite-sized pieces, discarding any tough cores, and finely chop the onion so it melts into the sauce. Grab a large, heavy-bottomed pot—stainless steel works best to avoid any metallic tang—and toss in the tomatoes, onion, and white vinegar.
2. Set the pot over medium-high heat and bring the mixture to a rolling boil, stirring every few minutes with a wooden spoon to keep it from sticking. You'll see the tomatoes start to release their juices, creating a soupy base.

3. Once boiling, drop the heat to medium-low. Let it simmer gently for 30 minutes, uncovered, stirring occasionally. The tomatoes will break down into a soft, pulpy mess—give them a little mash with your spoon if they're stubborn. You're looking for a consistency where the chunks are mostly gone.
4. Now, smooth it out. If you've got an immersion blender, stick it right in the pot and blend until velvety, being careful of hot splashes. No immersion blender? Let it cool slightly, then transfer in batches to a regular blender, pulsing until smooth before returning it to the pot.
5. With the puree back on the stove over medium-low heat, stir in the sugar, salt, pepper, cloves, and allspice. These spices give it that classic ketchup depth—don't skip 'em. Keep stirring to dissolve the sugar fully, then let it simmer uncovered for another 25-30 minutes. Stir every 5 minutes or so to prevent scorching as it thickens. You'll know it's ready when it coats the back of your spoon and holds a line when you drag a finger through it.
6. Taste it—adjust with a pinch more salt or a touch of sugar if it needs balancing. Let it cool for 10-15 minutes off the heat, then pour into sterilized jars or bottles using a funnel to keep it neat. Seal 'em up and pop in the fridge. It'll keep for a month, but I bet it won't last that long.

**Nutritional Facts (per 1 tbsp / 15 ml):**

- Calories: 15
- Fat: 0 g
- Carbs: 4 g (Sugars: 3 g)
- Protein: 0 g
- Sodium: 75 mg

## 2. Classic Mayonnaise

**Yield:** 1 cup (240 ml)

**Prep Time:** 10 minutes

### Ingredients:

- 1 large egg yolk (about 0.6 oz / 18 g)
- 1 tbsp (15 ml) lemon juice
- 1 tsp (5 g) Dijon mustard
- ¾ cup (180 ml) vegetable oil
- ¼ tsp (1 g) salt
- Pinch of ground white pepper (about 0.5 g)

### Instructions:

1. Set up a medium mixing bowl—glass or stainless steel works great—and add the egg yolk, lemon juice, and Dijon mustard. Grab a whisk (a sturdy one, not flimsy) and start whisking by hand to combine them into a smooth, pale yellow base. This takes about 30 seconds of good effort—get those ingredients friendly with each other.
2. Here's the tricky part: the oil. Measure it into a liquid measuring cup with a spout for control. Start by adding just a few drops—literally 2 or 3—to the yolk mixture, whisking constantly. You're building an emulsion, so go slow. Keep whisking until those drops disappear completely into the mix.
3. Add another few drops, whisking again until fully incorporated. Once you've used about a tablespoon of oil and the mixture looks thicker and creamier, you can pick

up the pace. Begin drizzling the oil in a thin, steady stream—think a pencil lead's width—while whisking nonstop. Your arm might protest, but don't stop; the mayo will break if you do.

4. As it thickens more (around the halfway mark), you'll see it turn glossy and hold soft peaks. Keep pouring the oil slowly until it's all in—should take about 5-7 minutes total. If it gets too thick to whisk, add a teaspoon of water to loosen it up, then continue.

5. Once all the oil's emulsified, stir in the salt and white pepper with a spoon—whisking's done its job. Taste it: want more zing? Add a few drops of lemon juice. Too bland? A pinch more salt. Transfer to a clean jar with a tight lid and chill in the fridge. Use within a week.

**Nutritional Facts (per 1 tbsp / 15 ml):**

- Calories: 90
- Fat: 10 g (Saturated: 1.5 g)
- Carbs: 0 g
- Protein: 0 g
- Sodium: 40 mg

### 3. Yellow Mustard

**Yield:** 1 cup (240 ml)

**Prep Time:** 10 minutes

**Cook Time:** 5 minutes + 24 hours resting

**Ingredients:**

- ½ cup (60 g) mustard powder
- ½ cup (120 ml) water
- ¼ cup (60 ml) white vinegar
- 1 tbsp (12 g) sugar
- 1 tsp (5 g) salt
- ¼ tsp (1 g) turmeric (for color)

**Instructions:**

1. Grab a small saucepan and measure the mustard powder into it—don't inhale too deep; it's pungent. Add the water, white vinegar, sugar, salt, and turmeric, then grab a whisk to combine everything into a smooth, bright yellow slurry. Make sure there are no clumps hiding in there.
2. Set the pan over medium heat and start stirring with a wooden spoon or heatproof spatula. Keep it moving as it warms up—you'll see it start to thicken slightly after 3-4 minutes. Don't let it boil; if bubbles form, lower the heat right away. Cook for about 5 minutes total, until it's a little pasty but still pourable.

3. Take it off the heat and let it sit in the pan for 10 minutes—it'll cool down and settle. Give it a good stir to check the consistency; it should look like a thin pudding at this point.
4. Pour the mustard into a clean glass jar using a small funnel or careful spoon work to avoid a mess. Seal it loosely with a lid or cover with a clean cloth secured by a rubber band—don't tighten it yet; it needs to breathe.
5. Let the jar sit on your counter at room temperature for 24 hours. This resting time mellows the sharpness of the mustard powder into that familiar tangy kick. After a day, give it a sniff and a taste—it'll be smoother than when you started. Tighten the lid and store in the fridge for up to 3 months.

**Nutritional Facts (per 1 tsp / 5 ml):**

- Calories: 5
- Fat: 0 g
- Carbs: 1 g (Sugars: 0.5 g)
- Protein: 0 g
- Sodium: 60 mg

## 4. Smoky Barbecue Sauce

**Yield:** 2 cups (480 ml)

**Prep Time:** 10 minutes

**Cook Time:** 20 minutes

**Ingredients:**

- 1 cup (240 ml) tomato puree
- ½ cup (120 ml) apple cider vinegar
- ¼ cup (50 g) brown sugar
- 2 tbsp (30 ml) molasses
- 1 tbsp (15 g) smoked paprika
- 1 tsp (5 g) garlic powder
- 1 tsp (5 g) onion powder
- ½ tsp (2 g) cayenne pepper
- Salt to taste (about 1 tsp / 5 g)

**Instructions:**

1. Measure out all your ingredients and have them ready—this moves fast once it starts. In a medium saucepan (one with a thick bottom is ideal), pour in the tomato puree, apple cider vinegar, brown sugar, and molasses. Add the smoked paprika, garlic powder, onion powder, cayenne, and salt.
2. Set the pan over medium heat and grab a wooden spoon. Stir everything together thoroughly, making sure the sugar and spices aren't clumped at the bottom—keep scraping

the edges as you go. Bring it to a gentle simmer, where you see small bubbles breaking the surface, about 5 minutes in.

3.  Drop the heat to low so it's just barely bubbling. Let it cook for 15-20 minutes, stirring every few minutes to prevent sticking or burning. The sauce will darken and thicken as the molasses and sugar meld with the tomato—watch for a glossy sheen and a consistency that coats your spoon without running off too quick.
4.  After 15 minutes, dip a clean spoon in and taste. Too mild? Add a pinch more cayenne. Too tart? A teaspoon of sugar. Adjust the salt last—it'll bring all the flavors together. If it's not thick enough, simmer 5 minutes more, but don't overdo it; it'll firm up as it cools.
5.  Take it off the heat and let it sit for 10 minutes in the pan, stirring once or twice as it cools. Pour into a jar or bottle using a funnel, then let it cool completely before sealing. Store in the fridge—it's good for a month.

**Nutritional Facts (per 2 tbsp / 30 ml):**

- Calories: 35
- Fat: 0 g
- Carbs: 8 g (Sugars: 7 g)
- Protein: 0 g
- Sodium: 150 mg

## 5. Fermented Red Hot Sauce

**Yield:** 1 cup (240 ml)

**Prep Time:** 15 minutes

**Fermentation Time:** 7-10 days

**Cook Time:** 10 minutes

### Ingredients:

- 1 lb (450 g) red chili peppers (e.g., Fresno), stemmed
- 2 cups (480 ml) water
- 1 tbsp (15 g) sea salt
- ¼ cup (60 ml) white vinegar

### Instructions:

1. Rinse your chili peppers under cold water, then pat dry with a clean towel. On a cutting board, slice off the stems and roughly chop the peppers into 1-inch pieces—seeds and all, unless you want it milder, then scoop some out. Pack them tightly into a clean quart-sized glass jar, leaving about 2 inches of headspace.
2. In a measuring cup, combine the water and sea salt, stirring with a spoon until the salt fully dissolves—this is your brine. Pour it over the peppers in the jar, making sure they're completely submerged. If they float, weigh them down with a small, clean glass weight or a zip-top bag filled with water.

3. Cover the jar's mouth with a clean cloth (like cheesecloth) and secure it with a rubber band—no lid yet; it needs air to ferment. Set it in a cool, dark spot—like a pantry or cupboard—for 7-10 days. Check daily: you'll see bubbles forming after a couple days, and it'll smell tangy. "Burp" it by gently pressing the peppers down with a clean spoon to release trapped gas.
4. After 7 days, taste a tiny bit of the brine with a clean spoon—it should be sharp and sour. If it's not tangy enough, let it go a few more days, up to 10. Once ready, pour the peppers and brine into a blender. Blend on high for 1-2 minutes until it's a smooth, fiery red puree—watch out for fumes!
5. Set a fine mesh sieve over a bowl and strain the puree, pressing with a spoon to push the liquid through. Discard the pulpy solids left behind. Stir the white vinegar into the strained sauce to brighten it up, then pour into a clean bottle or jar using a funnel. Seal and refrigerate—it'll keep for 6 months.

**Nutritional Facts (per 1 tsp / 5 ml):**

- Calories: 2
- Fat: 0 g
- Carbs: 0 g
- Protein: 0 g
- Sodium: 120 mg

## 6. Worcestershire Sauce

**Yield:** 1 cup (240 ml)

**Prep Time:** 15 minutes

**Cook Time:** 20 minutes + 2 weeks resting

### Ingredients:

- ½ cup (120 ml) apple cider vinegar
- ¼ cup (60 ml) soy sauce
- 2 tbsp (25 g) brown sugar
- 1 tbsp (15 ml) tamarind paste
- 1 tsp (5 g) anchovy paste
- ½ tsp (2 g) ground ginger
- ¼ tsp (1 g) ground cloves
- 1 small garlic clove (about 3 g), minced

### Instructions:

1. Prep your garlic first: peel and mince it finely so it blends in smooth. In a small saucepan, pour the apple cider vinegar and soy sauce, then add the brown sugar, tamarind paste, anchovy paste, ground ginger, ground cloves, and minced garlic.
2. Set the pan over medium heat and stir with a wooden spoon to combine everything. Keep stirring for a minute or two until the sugar dissolves and the pastes break down—you don't want any lumps. It'll smell strong and funky—don't worry, that's the umami building.

3. Bring it to a gentle simmer, where tiny bubbles just start to form around the edges. Lower the heat to medium-low and let it cook for 15-20 minutes, stirring every 5 minutes or so. The sauce will reduce slightly, darkening to a deep brown and thickening just enough to coat your spoon lightly.
4. Take it off the heat and let it cool in the pan for 5-10 minutes. Set a fine mesh sieve over a clean bowl or jar, then pour the sauce through, pressing with a spoon to get every last drop—discard the solids left behind.
5. Transfer the strained sauce to a glass jar with a lid using a funnel. Let it cool completely, then seal and pop it in the fridge. Shake it once a day for the first week, then let it rest for another week—2 weeks total—to let the flavors meld into that rich, savory punch. Keeps for 6 months chilled.

**Nutritional Facts (per 1 tsp / 5 ml):**

- Calories: 5
- Fat: 0 g
- Carbs: 1 g (Sugars: 1 g)
- Protein: 0 g
- Sodium: 130 mg

## 7. Garlic Aioli (Mayo Variation)
**Yield:** 1 cup (240 ml)

**Prep Time:** 15 minutes

**Ingredients:**

- 1 large egg yolk (about 0.6 oz / 18 g)
- 1 tbsp (15 ml) lemon juice
- 2 garlic cloves (about 6 g), minced
- ¾ cup (180 ml) olive oil
- ¼ tsp (1 g) salt

**Instructions:**

1. Peel and mince your garlic cloves finely—use a microplane if you've got one for extra smoothness. In a medium mixing bowl, combine the egg yolk, lemon juice, and minced garlic. Whisk by hand with a sturdy whisk for about 30 seconds until it's a uniform, pale mixture with little flecks of garlic.
2. Pour the olive oil into a spouted measuring cup for easy pouring. Start adding it to the bowl drop by drop—use your fingers or a small spoon if you need to—whisking constantly with your other hand. After about a tablespoon of oil is in and the mix starts to thicken, you'll feel it resist the whisk a bit—that's the emulsion kicking in.
3. Now, drizzle the oil in a thin, steady stream—slow as a trickle—while whisking nonstop. Keep your bowl steady; if it slides, set it on a damp towel. The aioli will grow creamier and thicker as you go—pause if your arm tires,

but don't stop mid-stream, or it might break. It'll take 7-10 minutes to use all the oil.

4. When the oil's fully incorporated, you'll have a glossy, thick spread that holds soft peaks. Stir in the salt with a spoon, then taste—add more lemon juice a drop at a time for brightness, or extra garlic if you're bold (just mince it super fine first).
5. Scrape the aioli into a clean jar with a tight lid, using a rubber spatula to get every bit. Chill in the fridge—it's best after an hour when the garlic mellows. Use within a week.

**Nutritional Facts (per 1 tbsp / 15 ml):**

- Calories: 95
- Fat: 10 g (Saturated: 1.5 g)
- Carbs: 0 g
- Protein: 0 g
- Sodium: 40 mg

## 8. Dijon Mustard

**Yield:** 1 cup (240 ml)

**Prep Time:** 10 minutes

**Cook Time:** 5 minutes + 48 hours resting

**Ingredients:**

- ½ cup (60 g) mustard seeds
- ½ cup (120 ml) white wine
- ¼ cup (60 ml) white vinegar
- 1 tsp (5 g) salt
- 1 tbsp (12 g) honey

**Instructions:**

1. The night before, measure the mustard seeds into a small bowl and pour in the white wine and white vinegar. Stir once with a spoon to wet all the seeds, then cover loosely with a cloth or plate and let sit at room temperature for 12-24 hours. They'll soften and soak up the liquid, getting plump and ready.
2. After soaking, pour the seeds and liquid into a blender or food processor. Add the salt and honey, then blend on medium-high for 1-2 minutes. Stop and scrape down the sides with a spatula—decide if you want it smooth (blend longer) or grainy (stop sooner). I like a bit of texture, but it's your call.

3. Scrape the mustard into a small saucepan and set it over low heat. Stir constantly with a wooden spoon as it warms—about 5 minutes—until it thickens slightly and smells fragrant. Don't let it boil; if it bubbles, pull it off the heat quick. You're just waking up the flavors here.
4. Remove from heat and let it cool in the pan for 10 minutes, giving it a stir now and then. Spoon it into a clean jar, using a funnel if you've got one, and seal loosely with a lid or cover with a cloth secured by a rubber band.
5. Let it sit at room temperature for 48 hours—this resting time smooths out the bite and deepens the taste. Stir it once halfway through, then taste after two days. Seal tight and refrigerate—it's good for 3 months.

**Nutritional Facts (per 1 tsp / 5 ml):**

- Calories: 10
- Fat: 0.5 g
- Carbs: 1 g (Sugars: 0.5 g)
- Protein: 0 g
- Sodium: 60 mg

## 9. Spicy Barbecue Sauce

**Yield:** 2 cups (480 ml)

**Prep Time:** 10 minutes

**Cook Time:** 20 minutes

**Ingredients:**

- 1 cup (240 ml) tomato puree
- ½ cup (120 ml) apple cider vinegar
- ¼ cup (50 g) brown sugar
- 2 tbsp (30 ml) hot sauce
- 1 tbsp (15 g) chili powder
- 1 tsp (5 g) garlic powder
- 1 tsp (5 g) smoked paprika
- ½ tsp (2 g) salt

**Instructions:**

1. Gather your ingredients and measure them into a medium saucepan—use one with a heavy bottom to avoid scorching. Pour in the tomato puree and apple cider vinegar, then add the brown sugar, hot sauce, chili powder, garlic powder, smoked paprika, and salt.
2. Set the pan over medium heat and stir with a wooden spoon to mix everything well. Keep stirring for a couple minutes until the sugar starts to dissolve and the spices blend into the liquid—you'll see it turn a rich, reddish-brown.

3. Bring it to a simmer—small bubbles should pop up across the surface after about 5 minutes. Reduce the heat to low, just enough to keep it gently bubbling, and cook for 15-20 minutes. Stir every 3-4 minutes, scraping the sides and bottom to prevent sticking. It'll thicken as it reduces, getting that sticky, saucy texture.
4. After 15 minutes, taste with a clean spoon. Too tame? Add a dash more hot sauce or chili powder. Too sharp? A pinch of sugar. Adjust salt last to tie it all together. If it's still too thin, simmer 5 more minutes—watch it close so it doesn't burn.
5. Pull it off the heat and let it cool in the pan for 10 minutes, stirring occasionally as it settles. Pour into a jar or bottle with a funnel, let it cool completely, then seal. Store in the fridge for up to a month.

**Nutritional Facts (per 2 tbsp / 30 ml):**

- Calories: 30
- Fat: 0 g
- Carbs: 7 g (Sugars: 6 g)
- Protein: 0 g
- Sodium: 140 mg

## 10. Sweet Pickle Relish

**Yield:** 2 cups (480 ml)

**Prep Time:** 20 minutes

**Cook Time:** 15 minutes

### Ingredients:

- 2 cups (300 g) finely chopped cucumbers
- ½ cup (75 g) finely chopped onion
- ½ cup (120 ml) white vinegar
- ¼ cup (50 g) sugar
- 1 tsp (5 g) salt
- ½ tsp (2 g) mustard seeds
- ¼ tsp (1 g) celery seeds

### Instructions:

1. Prep your veggies: rinse the cucumbers, then chop them into a fine dice—about ¼-inch pieces—so they cook evenly. Do the same with the onion. Measure them into a medium saucepan, then add the white vinegar, sugar, salt, mustard seeds, and celery seeds.
2. Set the pan over medium-high heat and stir with a wooden spoon to mix everything up. Keep stirring as it heats—about 3-5 minutes—until the sugar dissolves and the mixture starts to bubble vigorously. You'll smell the vinegar and spices waking up.

3. Once boiling, drop the heat to medium-low to keep a steady simmer. Cook for 10-15 minutes, stirring every few minutes. The liquid will reduce, and the cucumbers and onions will soften into a relish-like texture—soft but not mushy. If it looks dry before 10 minutes, add a tablespoon of water.
4. After 10 minutes, check the consistency—it should be thick and spoonable, with a bit of syrupy liquid left. Taste it: too tart? Add a teaspoon of sugar. Too bland? A pinch of salt. Simmer a few more minutes if it's too wet, but don't overcook or it'll lose that fresh bite.
5. Take it off the heat and let it cool in the pan for 10 minutes, stirring once or twice. Spoon into clean jars, using a funnel if you've got one, and let it cool completely before sealing. Store in the fridge—it's good for 2 months.

**Nutritional Facts (per 1 tbsp / 15 ml):**

- Calories: 10
- Fat: 0 g
- Carbs: 2 g (Sugars: 2 g)
- Protein: 0 g
- Sodium: 75 mg

---

This revised chapter dives deep into the preparation process, breaking each step into detailed, beginner-friendly actions while keeping Jasper's encouraging tone. The expanded instructions anticipate common pitfalls—like emulsions breaking or sauces scorching—and offer practical fixes, ensuring readers can confidently tackle these classics. Let me know if you'd like more adjustments!

## Chapter 2: Global Inspirations

The world's a big place, and I learned that best through its sauces. Every port I docked at in my Navy days had a flavor I couldn't shake—like the chimichurri I tasted in Buenos Aires. I was twenty-three, sunburned, and starving after a long shift, when a street vendor handed me a skewer of grilled beef drizzled with this green magic. It was garlicky, tangy, and so fresh it cut through the smoky meat like a breeze. I begged him for the recipe in broken Spanish, scribbling it on a napkin as he laughed and tossed in extra parsley. That moment stuck with me—proof that a sauce can carry you somewhere new, no passport needed. This chapter's my passport stamp collection: ten recipes from across the globe, each one a ticket to a far-off table.

## 1. Fresh Pico de Gallo (Mexico)

**Yield:** 2 cups (480 ml)

**Prep Time:** 15 minutes

### Ingredients:

- 1 lb (450 g) ripe tomatoes, diced
- ½ cup (75 g) finely chopped white onion
- ¼ cup (15 g) chopped fresh cilantro
- 1 jalapeño (about 1 oz / 28 g), seeded and minced
- 2 tbsp (30 ml) lime juice
- ½ tsp (2 g) salt

### Instructions:

1. Start with your tomatoes—pick ripe ones that smell sweet. Rinse them under cold water, then cut into ¼-inch dice on a cutting board, scooping out excess seeds if they're too juicy. Measure into a medium mixing bowl.
2. Peel and finely chop the onion—small pieces so they blend, not crunch. Add to the tomatoes. Rinse the cilantro, shake dry, and chop the leaves roughly—no stems, just the good stuff. Toss it in too.
3. Slice the jalapeño lengthwise, scrape out the seeds with a spoon (leave 'em if you like heat), and mince it fine—watch your hands; don't rub your eyes after. Add it to the bowl.
4. Pour in the lime juice and sprinkle the salt over everything. Grab a spoon and stir gently but thoroughly—fold from the

bottom up to mix without mashing the tomatoes. You want it chunky, not soupy.

5. Taste it: too mild? Add a pinch more jalapeño or salt. Too sharp? A teaspoon of sugar can soften it. Let it sit for 10 minutes on the counter to let the flavors meld, then serve fresh or jar it up—fridge it for up to 3 days.

**Nutritional Facts (per ¼ cup / 60 ml):**

- Calories: 20
- Fat: 0 g
- Carbs: 5 g (Sugars: 3 g)
- Protein: 1 g
- Sodium: 150 mg

## 2. Roasted Salsa Verde (Mexico)

**Yield:** 1.5 cups (360 ml)

**Prep Time:** 15 minutes

**Cook Time:** 20 minutes

### Ingredients:

- 1 lb (450 g) tomatillos, husked
- 1 jalapeño (about 1 oz / 28 g), stemmed
- 2 garlic cloves (about 6 g), unpeeled
- ½ cup (75 g) chopped white onion
- ¼ cup (15 g) chopped fresh cilantro
- 1 tbsp (15 ml) lime juice
- ½ tsp (2 g) salt

### Instructions:

1. Preheat your oven to 400°F (200°C). Peel the papery husks off the tomatillos and rinse them under warm water—they're sticky, so scrub gently. Pat dry, then place on a baking sheet with the jalapeño and unpeeled garlic cloves.
2. Roast for 15-20 minutes, flipping everything halfway with tongs. The tomatillos will soften and blister, the jalapeño will char slightly, and the garlic will smell nutty. Pull them out and let cool for 10 minutes on the sheet.
3. Peel the garlic once cool—pinch the skin off with your fingers. Slice the jalapeño open, scrape out seeds if you

want less heat, and roughly chop it. Toss the tomatillos, jalapeño, and garlic into a blender or food processor.
4. Add the chopped onion, cilantro, lime juice, and salt. Pulse 5-7 times for a chunky salsa, or blend 30 seconds for smooth—your choice. Scrape down the sides with a spatula if stuff sticks.
5. Pour into a bowl and taste—add more lime for zing or salt for balance. Let it cool completely, then transfer to a jar. Keeps in the fridge for a week.

**Nutritional Facts (per 2 tbsp / 30 ml):**

- Calories: 15
- Fat: 0 g
- Carbs: 3 g (Sugars: 2 g)
- Protein: 0 g
- Sodium: 100 mg

### 3. Chimichurri (Argentina)

**Yield:** 1 cup (240 ml)

**Prep Time:** 15 minutes

**Ingredients:**

- 1 cup (60 g) packed fresh parsley, finely chopped
- ¼ cup (15 g) fresh oregano, finely chopped
- 3 garlic cloves (about 9 g), minced
- ½ cup (120 ml) olive oil
- 2 tbsp (30 ml) red wine vinegar
- ½ tsp (2 g) red pepper flakes
- ½ tsp (2 g) salt

**Instructions:**

1. Rinse the parsley and oregano under cold water, then shake dry. Strip the leaves from the stems—discard the tough bits—and chop finely on a cutting board. You want them small but not mushy; aim for a confetti-like pile. Scoop into a medium bowl.
2. Peel and mince the garlic—use a sharp knife or microplane for a fine texture. Add it to the herbs. Measure the olive oil and red wine vinegar into the bowl, then sprinkle in the red pepper flakes and salt.
3. Stir everything with a fork or small whisk—really work it to blend the oil and vinegar with the herbs. Keep going for a minute until it looks cohesive, not separated. You're after a loose, spoonable sauce, not a paste.

4. Taste it on a clean spoon—too mild? Add more pepper flakes. Too sharp? A drizzle of oil. Let it sit for 15 minutes at room temp—the garlic and herbs will bloom—then stir again before jarring. Fridge it for up to 2 weeks; shake before using.

**Nutritional Facts (per 1 tbsp / 15 ml):**

- Calories: 60
- Fat: 7 g (Saturated: 1 g)
- Carbs: 1 g
- Protein: 0 g
- Sodium: 75 mg

## 4. Harissa (North Africa)

**Yield:** 1 cup (240 ml)

**Prep Time:** 20 minutes

**Cook Time:** 10 minutes

**Ingredients:**

- 10 dried red chilies (about 2 oz / 56 g), stemmed and seeded
- 1 tsp (5 g) caraway seeds
- 1 tsp (5 g) coriander seeds
- ½ tsp (2 g) cumin seeds
- 3 garlic cloves (about 9 g), peeled
- ½ cup (120 ml) olive oil
- 1 tsp (5 g) salt

**Instructions:**

1. Fill a small bowl with hot water and soak the dried chilies for 15 minutes—they'll soften up. While they soak, toast the caraway, coriander, and cumin seeds in a dry skillet over medium heat. Shake the pan for 2-3 minutes until they smell fragrant, then grind them in a spice grinder or mortar and pestle into a fine powder.
2. Drain the chilies, pat dry with a towel, and roughly chop them—watch your hands; they're spicy. Toss the chilies, ground spices, peeled garlic, olive oil, and salt into a blender or food processor.

3. Blend on high for 1-2 minutes, stopping to scrape down the sides with a spatula. You want a thick, slightly grainy paste—smooth is fine too, just blend longer if that's your style. If it's too thick to move, add a tablespoon of water and pulse again.
4. Scrape the harissa into a small saucepan and set over low heat. Cook for 5-7 minutes, stirring constantly with a wooden spoon—it'll deepen in color and smell smoky. Don't let it burn; keep the heat gentle.
5. Cool it in the pan for 10 minutes, then taste—add salt or a splash of oil if it needs rounding out. Spoon into a jar, cover with a thin layer of olive oil to seal, and refrigerate for up to a month.

**Nutritional Facts (per 1 tbsp / 15 ml):**

- Calories: 70
- Fat: 7 g (Saturated: 1 g)
- Carbs: 2 g (Sugars: 1 g)
- Protein: 0 g
- Sodium: 150 mg

## 5. Soy-Based Dipping Sauce (Japan)
**Yield:** ½ cup (120 ml)

**Prep Time:** 10 minutes

**Ingredients:**

- ¼ cup (60 ml) soy sauce
- 2 tbsp (30 ml) rice vinegar
- 1 tbsp (15 ml) mirin
- 1 tsp (5 g) grated fresh ginger
- 1 tsp (5 g) sesame seeds
- 1 green onion (about 10 g), thinly sliced

**Instructions:**

1. Measure the soy sauce, rice vinegar, and mirin into a small bowl—use a liquid measuring cup for accuracy. Stir with a spoon to combine the liquids into a dark, glossy base.
2. Peel a small knob of ginger and grate it finely—use a microplane or the small holes of a box grater—straight into the bowl. Aim for a teaspoon; too much can overpower it. Stir it in well so it disperses.
3. Toast the sesame seeds in a dry skillet over medium heat for 1-2 minutes—shake the pan until they're golden and nutty. Tip them into the sauce and stir again.
4. Rinse the green onion, trim the ends, and slice it thin—white and green parts both—and add to the mix. Stir gently to distribute everything evenly; you want flecks of color and texture.

5. Taste it—too salty? Add a splash of water. Too tame? A pinch more ginger. Let it sit for 5 minutes to meld, then pour into a small jar or serve right away. Keeps in the fridge for a week.

**Nutritional Facts (per 1 tbsp / 15 ml):**

- Calories: 10
- Fat: 0 g
- Carbs: 1 g (Sugars: 1 g)
- Protein: 1 g
- Sodium: 450 mg

### 6. Tzatziki (Greece)

**Yield:** 2 cups (480 ml)

**Prep Time:** 20 minutes

**Ingredients:**

- 1 cup (240 g) Greek yogurt
- 1 cucumber (about 8 oz / 225 g), grated
- 2 garlic cloves (about 6 g), minced
- 1 tbsp (15 ml) olive oil
- 1 tbsp (15 ml) lemon juice
- 1 tsp (5 g) chopped fresh dill
- ½ tsp (2 g) salt

**Instructions:**

1. Rinse the cucumber, then grate it using the large holes of a box grater—skin and all—into a colander set over a bowl. Sprinkle with a pinch of salt and let it sit for 10 minutes; it'll release water. Press down with your hands or a spoon to squeeze out as much liquid as you can—discard the juice.
2. Scoop the Greek yogurt into a medium bowl—full-fat's best for creaminess. Add the drained cucumber and stir with a spoon to mix it in evenly.
3. Peel and mince the garlic finely—almost to a paste—and add it to the bowl. Pour in the olive oil and lemon juice, then sprinkle in the chopped dill and salt.
4. Stir everything together thoroughly—really work it for a minute so the flavors blend and the texture's smooth but

still chunky from the cucumber. Taste it: need more zip? Add a splash of lemon. Too thick? A tablespoon of water.

5. Cover the bowl and chill for 30 minutes in the fridge to let it set, then transfer to a jar. Keeps for 5 days refrigerated—stir before serving.

**Nutritional Facts (per 2 tbsp / 30 ml):**

- Calories: 25
- Fat: 1.5 g (Saturated: 0.5 g)
- Carbs: 1 g (Sugars: 1 g)
- Protein: 2 g
- Sodium: 80 mg

## 7. Sriracha (Thailand)

**Yield:** 1.5 cups (360 ml)

**Prep Time:** 20 minutes

**Fermentation Time:** 5-7 days

**Cook Time:** 15 minutes

**Ingredients:**

- 1 lb (450 g) red chili peppers, stemmed
- 3 garlic cloves (about 9 g), peeled
- 2 tbsp (25 g) sugar
- 1 tbsp (15 g) salt
- ½ cup (120 ml) white vinegar

**Instructions:**

1. Rinse the chili peppers, pat dry, and chop them roughly—seeds in for heat, out for milder. Toss into a blender with the peeled garlic, sugar, and salt. Pulse 5-7 times until it's a coarse puree—don't overdo it yet.
2. Scrape the mixture into a clean quart jar, leaving space at the top. Cover with a cloth secured by a rubber band and set in a dark, cool spot for 5-7 days. Check daily—stir with a clean spoon and look for bubbles; it'll smell tangy by day 3 or 4.
3. After fermentation (taste the mix—it'll be sharp and funky), pour it back into the blender. Add the white vinegar and

blend on high for 1-2 minutes until smooth—scrape the sides if needed.

4. Pour the puree into a small saucepan and set over medium heat. Bring to a simmer, stirring with a wooden spoon, and cook for 10-15 minutes—stir often as it thickens and darkens. Watch for splatters; lower the heat if it gets wild.

5. Cool it in the pan for 10 minutes, then strain through a fine mesh sieve into a bowl, pressing with a spoon. Bottle the smooth sauce—discard solids—and refrigerate for up to 6 months.

**Nutritional Facts (per 1 tsp / 5 ml):**

- Calories: 5
- Fat: 0 g
- Carbs: 1 g (Sugars: 1 g)
- Protein: 0 g
- Sodium: 100 mg

## 8. Gochujang (Korea)

**Yield:** 2 cups (480 ml)

**Prep Time:** 30 minutes

**Fermentation Time:** 2 weeks

### Ingredients:

- 1 cup (120 g) gochugaru (Korean red pepper flakes)
- ½ cup (100 g) sweet rice flour
- ¼ cup (50 g) sugar
- ¼ cup (60 ml) soy sauce
- 2 tbsp (30 g) salt
- 2 cups (480 ml) water

### Instructions:

1. In a medium saucepan, whisk the sweet rice flour and water until smooth—no lumps. Set over medium heat and stir constantly with a wooden spoon for 5-7 minutes—it'll thicken into a sticky paste. Cool it in the pan for 15 minutes.
2. Once lukewarm, stir in the gochugaru, sugar, soy sauce, and salt—mix well until it's a vibrant red paste. It'll feel gritty; that's normal. Scrape into a wide, shallow glass container—more surface area helps fermentation.
3. Cover with a cloth and secure with a rubber band. Set in a cool, dark spot for 2 weeks—stir daily with a clean spoon.

It'll bubble and smell spicy-sweet after a few days; keep it going until it's tangy and rich.
4. After 2 weeks, taste it—should be bold and complex. If it's not there yet, give it a few more days. Spoon into a jar, pressing down to remove air pockets, and seal with a lid.
5. Refrigerate—it's good for months, but let it sit a day before using to settle. Stir well before scooping out.

**Nutritional Facts (per 1 tbsp / 15 ml):**

- Calories: 20
- Fat: 0 g
- Carbs: 4 g (Sugars: 2 g)
- Protein: 1 g
- Sodium: 300 mg

### 9. Peri-Peri Sauce (South Africa)

**Yield:** 1 cup (240 ml)

**Prep Time:** 20 minutes

**Cook Time:** 15 minutes

**Ingredients:**

- 10 bird's eye chilies (about 2 oz / 56 g), stemmed
- 1 red bell pepper (about 6 oz / 170 g), chopped
- 3 garlic cloves (about 9 g), peeled
- ¼ cup (60 ml) olive oil
- 2 tbsp (30 ml) lemon juice
- 1 tsp (5 g) smoked paprika
- ½ tsp (2 g) salt

**Instructions:**

1. Rinse the chilies and bell pepper. Chop the chilies roughly—seeds in for fire—and the bell pepper into 1-inch chunks. Toss them into a blender with the peeled garlic, olive oil, lemon juice, smoked paprika, and salt.
2. Blend on high for 1-2 minutes until smooth—stop and scrape the sides with a spatula if it sticks. You're aiming for a bright orange-red puree with no big chunks.
3. Pour the mixture into a small saucepan and set over medium heat. Bring to a simmer, stirring with a wooden spoon—it'll bubble gently after 3-5 minutes. Lower the

heat to medium-low and cook for 10 minutes, stirring often; it'll thicken slightly and smell smoky-spicy.
4. Cool it in the pan for 10 minutes—give it a stir now and then. Taste: too hot? Add a teaspoon of oil. Too tame? More chilies next time. Pour into a jar using a funnel and let it cool completely before sealing.
5. Refrigerate for up to a month—shake well before using; the oil might separate.

**Nutritional Facts (per 1 tbsp / 15 ml):**

- Calories: 40
- Fat: 4 g (Saturated: 0.5 g)
- Carbs: 2 g (Sugars: 1 g)
- Protein: 0 g
- Sodium: 75 mg

## 10. Thai Peanut Sauce (Thailand)

**Yield:** 1.5 cups (360 ml)

**Prep Time:** 15 minutes

**Cook Time:** 10 minutes

**Ingredients:**

- ½ cup (120 g) creamy peanut butter
- ¼ cup (60 ml) coconut milk
- 2 tbsp (30 ml) soy sauce
- 1 tbsp (15 ml) lime juice
- 1 tbsp (12 g) brown sugar
- 1 tsp (5 g) red curry paste
- ½ cup (120 ml) water

**Instructions:**

1. Measure the peanut butter into a small saucepan—natural works best, but any creamy kind's fine. Add the coconut milk, soy sauce, lime juice, brown sugar, red curry paste, and water.
2. Set over medium-low heat and stir with a whisk—start slow to blend the peanut butter into the liquids. Keep whisking for 2-3 minutes as it warms; it'll look lumpy at first, then smooth out into a thick, creamy mix.
3. Bring it to a gentle simmer—tiny bubbles should form around the edges—about 5 minutes in. Cook for another 5 minutes, stirring constantly with a wooden spoon to

prevent sticking or scorching. It'll thicken to a dip-able consistency.
4. Pull it off the heat and let it cool in the pan for 10 minutes—stir occasionally as it sets. Taste: too thick? Add a splash of water. Too mild? More curry paste. Pour into a jar and cool completely before sealing.
5. Refrigerate for up to 2 weeks—warm it gently before serving if it firms up too much.

**Nutritional Facts (per 2 tbsp / 30 ml):**

- Calories: 90
- Fat: 7 g (Saturated: 2 g)
- Carbs: 4 g (Sugars: 2 g)
- Protein: 3 g
- Sodium: 200 mg

## Chapter 3: Sweet & Savory Spreads

Some flavors don't fit neatly into boxes—they dance between sweet and savory, making everything they touch a little more interesting. Take caramelized onion jam—it's my kind of troublemaker. I stumbled into it years back in Austin, hosting a barbecue that was spiraling fast. The ribs were overdone, the guests were late, and I was scrambling. I'd been slow-cooking onions for hours, mostly out of habit, when I tossed in some sugar and vinegar on a whim. By the time folks showed up, that jam was slathered on everything—ribs, bread, even a spoon or two straight from the jar. They raved, and I learned a lesson: a good spread can save the day and steal the show. This chapter's full of those in-between gems—ten recipes to smear, dollop, or dip, blurring the lines in the best way.

# 1. Honey Mustard

**Yield:** 1 cup (240 ml)

**Prep Time:** 10 minutes

## Ingredients:

- ½ cup (120 g) Dijon mustard
- ¼ cup (60 ml) honey
- 2 tbsp (30 ml) apple cider vinegar
- 1 tbsp (15 ml) olive oil
- ¼ tsp (1 g) ground black pepper

## Instructions:

1. Grab a medium mixing bowl—glass or stainless steel keeps it neutral—and measure in the Dijon mustard. Spoon the honey right on top—it'll be sticky, so scrape the spoon clean with a spatula.
2. Pour in the apple cider vinegar and olive oil, then sprinkle the black pepper over the lot. Pick up a whisk—something sturdy—and start blending. Whisk briskly for about a minute, working from the center out, until the honey dissolves and the mixture looks smooth and glossy.
3. If the honey clumps, keep whisking—dip the bowl in a shallow pan of warm water for 30 seconds if it's stubborn,

then try again. You're aiming for a thick, creamy spread that holds together without separating.

4. Taste it with a clean spoon—too sharp? Add a teaspoon more honey. Too sweet? A splash of vinegar. Stir again after adjusting to make sure it's even.

5. Scrape it into a clean jar with a tight lid, using a rubber spatula to get every bit. Let it sit at room temperature for 10 minutes to settle the flavors, then pop it in the fridge—it's good for a month.

**Nutritional Facts (per 1 tbsp / 15 ml):**

- Calories: 35
- Fat: 1 g (Saturated: 0 g)
- Carbs: 6 g (Sugars: 5 g)
- Protein: 0 g
- Sodium: 120 mg

## 2. Spiced Apple Chutney

**Yield:** 2 cups (480 ml)

**Prep Time:** 20 minutes

**Cook Time:** 40 minutes

**Ingredients:**

- 2 lbs (900 g) apples, peeled and chopped
- ½ cup (100 g) brown sugar
- ½ cup (120 ml) apple cider vinegar
- ¼ cup (40 g) raisins
- 1 small onion (about 4 oz / 113 g), finely chopped
- 1 tsp (5 g) ground cinnamon
- ½ tsp (2 g) ground ginger
- ¼ tsp (1 g) ground cloves

**Instructions:**

1. Peel the apples with a paring knife, core them, and chop into ½-inch pieces—keep 'em rustic. Measure into a large, heavy-bottomed pot. Finely chop the onion so it melts into the mix, and add it too.
2. Pour in the brown sugar, apple cider vinegar, and toss in the raisins, cinnamon, ginger, and cloves. Stir with a

wooden spoon over medium heat until the sugar starts to dissolve—about 3-5 minutes—and the apples release a little juice.

3. Bring it to a simmer—small bubbles should pop up—then drop the heat to low. Cook uncovered for 35-40 minutes, stirring every 5-10 minutes. The apples will soften and break down, and the liquid will thicken into a syrupy jam—scrape the bottom to prevent sticking.

4. After 30 minutes, check the texture—mash a few apple chunks with your spoon if you want it smoother. Keep cooking until it's thick enough to mound on a spoon; if it's too runny, simmer 5 more minutes.

5. Taste it—too tart? Add a tablespoon of sugar. Too mild? A pinch of ginger. Let it cool in the pot for 15 minutes, stirring occasionally, then spoon into sterilized jars with a funnel. Seal and refrigerate for up to 2 months.

**Nutritional Facts (per 2 tbsp / 30 ml):**

- Calories: 50
- Fat: 0 g
- Carbs: 13 g (Sugars: 11 g)
- Protein: 0 g
- Sodium: 5 mg

### 3. Caramelized Onion Jam

**Yield:** 1.5 cups (360 ml)

**Prep Time:** 15 minutes

**Cook Time:** 1 hour

**Ingredients:**

- 2 lbs (900 g) yellow onions, thinly sliced
- 2 tbsp (30 ml) olive oil
- ¼ cup (50 g) brown sugar
- ¼ cup (60 ml) balsamic vinegar
- ½ tsp (2 g) salt
- ¼ tsp (1 g) ground black pepper

**Instructions:**

1. Peel the onions and slice them thin—use a sharp knife or mandoline for even ⅛-inch rings. Heat the olive oil in a large skillet—cast iron's perfect—over medium heat until it shimmers, then add the onions all at once.
2. Stir with a wooden spoon to coat them in oil, then let them cook for 10 minutes undisturbed—they'll soften and shrink. Lower the heat to medium-low and cook for 30-40

minutes more, stirring every 5-10 minutes. They'll turn golden, then deep brown—don't rush it; slow is the secret.

3. When they're sticky and caramelized, sprinkle in the brown sugar, balsamic vinegar, salt, and pepper. Stir well to dissolve the sugar and deglaze the pan—scrape up those browned bits from the bottom; they're gold.

4. Cook for another 10-15 minutes, stirring often, until it's a thick, jammy mess—liquid should mostly evaporate, leaving a glossy spread. If it sticks, add a tablespoon of water and keep going.

5. Taste—need more tang? A splash of vinegar. Too sweet? A pinch of salt. Cool in the skillet for 10 minutes, then transfer to a jar with a spatula. Refrigerate for up to 3 weeks.

**Nutritional Facts (per 1 tbsp / 15 ml):**

- Calories: 40
- Fat: 1 g (Saturated: 0 g)
- Carbs: 7 g (Sugars: 5 g)
- Protein: 0 g
- Sodium: 50 mg

## 4. Fig and Balsamic Reduction

**Yield:** 1 cup (240 ml)

**Prep Time:** 15 minutes

**Cook Time:** 25 minutes

**Ingredients:**

- 1 cup (150 g) dried figs, chopped
- ½ cup (120 ml) balsamic vinegar
- ¼ cup (50 g) sugar
- ½ cup (120 ml) water
- ¼ tsp (1 g) ground black pepper

**Instructions:**

1. Chop the dried figs into small pieces—about ¼-inch—removing any tough stems. Toss them into a small saucepan with the balsamic vinegar, sugar, water, and black pepper.
2. Set over medium heat and stir with a wooden spoon until the sugar dissolves—about 3-5 minutes. The figs will start to plump as the liquid warms; keep stirring to coat them evenly.

3. Bring to a gentle simmer—small bubbles around the edges—then reduce heat to low. Cook for 20-25 minutes, stirring every 5 minutes. The figs will soften into a paste, and the liquid will reduce to a thick, syrupy glaze—watch it close; it thickens fast near the end.

4. If it's too chunky, mash the figs with a fork or blend briefly with an immersion blender—leave some texture if you like. Cook a few more minutes if it's too thin; it should cling to the spoon.

5. Taste—too sweet? Add a splash of vinegar. Too tart? A teaspoon of sugar. Cool in the pan for 10 minutes, stirring occasionally, then pour into a jar with a funnel. Refrigerate for up to a month.

**Nutritional Facts (per 1 tbsp / 15 ml):**

- Calories: 45
- Fat: 0 g
- Carbs: 11 g (Sugars: 9 g)
- Protein: 0 g
- Sodium: 5 mg

## 5. Sweet Chili Sauce

**Yield:** 1.5 cups (360 ml)

**Prep Time:** 15 minutes

**Cook Time:** 20 minutes

**Ingredients:**

- ½ cup (120 ml) rice vinegar
- ½ cup (100 g) sugar
- ¼ cup (60 ml) water
- 2 red chilies (about 1 oz / 28 g), finely chopped
- 2 garlic cloves (about 6 g), minced
- 1 tbsp (8 g) cornstarch
- 2 tbsp (30 ml) water (for slurry)

**Instructions:**

1. Measure the rice vinegar, sugar, and ¼ cup water into a small saucepan. Finely chop the chilies—seeds in for heat—and mince the garlic; add both to the pan.
2. Set over medium heat and stir with a wooden spoon until the sugar dissolves—about 3-5 minutes. Bring to a simmer, stirring occasionally, and let it bubble gently for 10 minutes—the chilies will soften, and it'll smell sweet-spicy.

3. In a small bowl, whisk the cornstarch with 2 tablespoons water until smooth—no lumps. Pour this slurry into the simmering sauce, stirring constantly. It'll thicken fast—keep stirring for 2-3 minutes until it's glossy and coats the spoon.
4. Check the texture—too thin? Simmer 2 more minutes. Too thick? Add a tablespoon of water and stir. Taste—need more kick? Add chili flakes. Too tart? A pinch of sugar.
5. Cool in the pan for 10 minutes, stirring now and then, then pour into a jar with a funnel. Let it cool completely before sealing—refrigerate for up to 2 months.

**Nutritional Facts (per 1 tbsp / 15 ml):**

- Calories: 30
- Fat: 0 g
- Carbs: 8 g (Sugars: 7 g)
- Protein: 0 g
- Sodium: 0 mg

## 6. Blackberry Sage Jam

**Yield:** 2 cups (480 ml)

**Prep Time:** 15 minutes

**Cook Time:** 30 minutes

**Ingredients:**

- 2 cups (300 g) fresh blackberries
- 1 cup (200 g) sugar
- 2 tbsp (30 ml) lemon juice
- 1 tbsp (5 g) finely chopped fresh sage
- ¼ cup (60 ml) water

**Instructions:**

1. Rinse the blackberries under cold water, pat dry, and toss into a medium saucepan. Add the sugar, lemon juice, chopped sage, and water—stir gently with a wooden spoon to coat the berries.
2. Set over medium heat and stir occasionally as it warms—about 5 minutes—until the sugar dissolves and the berries start to burst. Mash them lightly with a potato masher or the back of your spoon; leave some chunks for texture.

3. Bring to a simmer—bubbles will foam up—then lower heat to medium-low. Cook for 25-30 minutes, stirring every 5 minutes. Skim off any foam with a spoon—it'll thicken into a loose jam that clings to the spoon.
4. Check after 20 minutes—too runny? Keep cooking. Too thick? Add a tablespoon of water. Taste—more sage for earthiness, or lemon for brightness, if needed.
5. Cool in the pan for 15 minutes, stirring occasionally, then spoon into jars with a funnel. Seal and refrigerate for up to a month.

**Nutritional Facts (per 1 tbsp / 15 ml):**

- Calories: 35
- Fat: 0 g
- Carbs: 9 g (Sugars: 8 g)
- Protein: 0 g
- Sodium: 0 mg

## 7. Maple Bacon Spread

**Yield:** 1 cup (240 ml)

**Prep Time:** 20 minutes

**Cook Time:** 25 minutes

**Ingredients:**

- 6 slices bacon (about 6 oz / 170 g), chopped
- ¼ cup (60 ml) maple syrup
- 2 tbsp (25 g) brown sugar
- 2 tbsp (30 ml) apple cider vinegar
- ¼ tsp (1 g) ground black pepper

**Instructions:**

1. Chop the bacon into small pieces—¼-inch bits—and toss into a cold skillet. Set over medium heat and cook for 10-15 minutes, stirring with a wooden spoon, until crispy and browned—don't burn it. Drain on paper towels, keeping 1 tablespoon of fat in the pan.
2. Return the skillet to medium heat and add the maple syrup, brown sugar, apple cider vinegar, and black pepper to the bacon fat. Stir until the sugar dissolves—about 2-3 minutes—and it starts to bubble.

3. Add the bacon back in and stir to coat. Cook for 5-10 minutes, stirring often, until it thickens into a sticky, jam-like spread—the liquid will reduce and cling to the bacon.
4. Taste—too sweet? A splash of vinegar. Too mild? More pepper. If it's too loose, cook a few minutes more; it firms up as it cools.
5. Cool in the skillet for 10 minutes, then scrape into a jar with a spatula. Refrigerate for up to 2 weeks—warm slightly before serving if it hardens.

**Nutritional Facts (per 1 tbsp / 15 ml):**

- Calories: 60
- Fat: 3 g (Saturated: 1 g)
- Carbs: 6 g (Sugars: 5 g)
- Protein: 2 g
- Sodium: 150 mg

## 8. Cranberry Orange Relish

**Yield:** 2 cups (480 ml)

**Prep Time:** 15 minutes

**Cook Time:** 15 minutes

**Ingredients:**

- 2 cups (200 g) fresh cranberries
- 1 orange (about 6 oz / 170 g), zested and juiced
- ¾ cup (150 g) sugar
- ¼ cup (60 ml) water
- ¼ tsp (1 g) ground cinnamon

**Instructions:**

1. Rinse the cranberries and pick out any mushy ones. Zest the orange with a microplane—get all the bright stuff—then juice it into a measuring cup (should be about ¼ cup). Toss both into a medium saucepan with the cranberries, sugar, water, and cinnamon.
2. Set over medium heat and stir with a wooden spoon until the sugar dissolves—about 3-5 minutes. The cranberries will start to pop as it heats; keep stirring gently to help them along.

3. Bring to a simmer and cook for 10-15 minutes—stir every few minutes. It'll thicken as the cranberries break down into a chunky relish; if you want it smoother, mash with a spoon near the end.

4. Taste—too tart? Add a tablespoon of sugar. Too sweet? A squeeze of lemon juice. Cool in the pan for 10 minutes, stirring occasionally, then spoon into jars with a funnel. Refrigerate for up to a month.

**Nutritional Facts (per 2 tbsp / 30 ml):**

- Calories: 45
- Fat: 0 g
- Carbs: 12 g (Sugars: 10 g)
- Protein: 0 g
- Sodium: 0 mg

## 9. Roasted Garlic and Honey Spread

**Yield:** 1 cup (240 ml)

**Prep Time:** 10 minutes

**Cook Time:** 45 minutes

**Ingredients:**

- 2 heads garlic (about 4 oz / 113 g)
- ½ cup (120 ml) honey
- 1 tbsp (15 ml) olive oil
- ¼ tsp (1 g) salt
- ¼ tsp (1 g) ground black pepper

**Instructions:**

1. Preheat your oven to 400°F (200°C). Slice the top off each garlic head to expose the cloves—don't peel. Place them cut-side up on a sheet of foil, drizzle with olive oil, and sprinkle with salt and pepper. Wrap tightly and roast for 40-45 minutes—cloves will be soft and golden.
2. Let the garlic cool for 10 minutes, then squeeze the cloves out of their skins into a small bowl—use your fingers or a fork; they'll pop right out. Mash them with a fork into a smooth paste.

3. Measure the honey into a small saucepan and set over low heat. Add the mashed garlic and stir with a wooden spoon for 2-3 minutes—it'll warm and blend into a thick, spreadable mix.
4. Taste—need more bite? A pinch of pepper. Too strong? More honey. Cook a minute more if it's too thin; it'll firm up as it cools.
5. Cool in the pan for 10 minutes, then scrape into a jar with a spatula. Refrigerate for up to a month—let it soften at room temp before spreading.

**Nutritional Facts (per 1 tbsp / 15 ml):**

- Calories: 50
- Fat: 1 g (Saturated: 0 g)
- Carbs: 11 g (Sugars: 10 g)
- Protein: 0 g
- Sodium: 30 mg

## 10. Apricot Rosemary Jam

**Yield:** 2 cups (480 ml)

**Prep Time:** 15 minutes

**Cook Time:** 30 minutes

### Ingredients:

- 2 cups (300 g) dried apricots, chopped
- 1 cup (200 g) sugar
- ½ cup (120 ml) water
- 2 tbsp (30 ml) lemon juice
- 1 tsp (5 g) finely chopped fresh rosemary

### Instructions:

1. Chop the dried apricots into small pieces—¼-inch bits—and toss into a medium saucepan. Add the sugar, water, lemon juice, and chopped rosemary—rinse the rosemary first and strip leaves from the stem.
2. Set over medium heat and stir with a wooden spoon until the sugar dissolves—about 5 minutes. The apricots will start to soften as the liquid warms; keep stirring to coat them evenly.

3. Bring to a simmer—bubbles will form—and lower heat to medium-low. Cook for 25-30 minutes, stirring every 5 minutes. The apricots will break down into a thick jam—mash with a spoon if you want it smoother; it'll thicken more as it cools.
4. Taste—too sweet? Add a splash of lemon. Need more herb? A pinch of rosemary. If it's too runny, cook 5 more minutes—watch it close near the end.
5. Cool in the pan for 15 minutes, stirring occasionally, then spoon into jars with a funnel. Seal and refrigerate for up to 2 months.

**Nutritional Facts (per 1 tbsp / 15 ml):**

- Calories: 40
- Fat: 0 g
- Carbs: 10 g (Sugars: 9 g)
- Protein: 0 g
- Sodium: 0 mg

## Chapter 4: Creamy Creations

There's a comfort in creamy sauces that's hard to beat—they wrap around a dish like a hug. I learned that with ranch dressing, back when I was a kid sneaking into Grandma Eula's fridge. She'd whip up a batch for Sunday supper, tangy and herby, and I'd dip anything I could find—carrots, chicken wings, even a stray biscuit—until she caught me with a grin and a swat. "Save some for the table, Jasper!" she'd say. That ranch wasn't just a dip; it was her way of making everything taste like home. This chapter's all about that richness—ten creamy recipes to spoon, drizzle, or dunk, each one a little bit of comfort you can make yourself.

# 1. Classic Ranch Dressing

**Yield:** 1.5 cups (360 ml)

**Prep Time:** 15 minutes

**Ingredients:**

- ½ cup (120 g) mayonnaise
- ½ cup (120 g) sour cream
- ¼ cup (60 ml) buttermilk
- 1 tsp (5 g) garlic powder
- 1 tsp (5 g) onion powder
- 1 tbsp (5 g) chopped fresh dill
- 1 tbsp (5 g) chopped fresh parsley
- ½ tsp (2 g) salt

**Instructions:**

1. Scoop the mayonnaise and sour cream into a medium mixing bowl—use a rubber spatula to get it all. Pour in the buttermilk—it'll thin things out—and stir with a whisk until smooth, about 30 seconds; no lumps allowed.
2. Measure the garlic powder and onion powder into the bowl—tap the spoons to level them off. Rinse the dill and parsley, pat dry with a towel, and chop them fine—no big

chunks; you want flecks of green. Add them in with the salt.

3. Whisk everything together briskly for a minute—work from the center out to blend the powders and herbs evenly. Scrape the sides with your spatula to make sure nothing's hiding, then whisk again until it's creamy and uniform.

4. Taste it on a clean spoon—too thick? Add a tablespoon more buttermilk. Too bland? A pinch more salt or herbs. Keep tweaking until it's tangy and bright.

5. Scrape into a jar with a tight lid, using the spatula to get every drop. Chill in the fridge for 30 minutes to let the flavors meld—shake or stir before serving. Keeps for a week.

**Nutritional Facts (per 2 tbsp / 30 ml):**

- Calories: 90
- Fat: 9 g (Saturated: 2 g)
- Carbs: 1 g (Sugars: 1 g)
- Protein: 1 g
- Sodium: 180 mg

## 2. Herbed Ranch Dressing (Variation)

**Yield:** 1.5 cups (360 ml)

**Prep Time:** 15 minutes

**Ingredients:**

- ½ cup (120 g) mayonnaise
- ½ cup (120 g) Greek yogurt
- ¼ cup (60 ml) milk
- 1 tsp (5 g) dried chives
- 1 tsp (5 g) dried thyme
- 1 tsp (5 g) garlic powder
- 1 tbsp (5 g) chopped fresh parsley
- ½ tsp (2 g) salt

**Instructions:**

1. Measure the mayonnaise and Greek yogurt into a medium bowl—scoop carefully to avoid air pockets. Pour in the milk to loosen it up, then stir with a whisk for 30 seconds until it's smooth and creamy—no streaks of yogurt left.
2. Add the dried chives, thyme, and garlic powder—sprinkle them evenly over the top. Rinse the parsley, shake dry, and chop it fine; toss it in with the salt. Grab your whisk again and blend everything together for a solid

minute—get those herbs worked in so they're not clumped.

3. Scrape the sides with a spatula and whisk once more—look for a thick, pourable dressing that coats the whisk lightly. If it's too stiff, drizzle in a teaspoon of milk and mix again.

4. Dip a spoon in—too mild? Add a pinch more thyme or salt. Too thin? A dollop of yogurt. Adjust until it sings, then transfer to a jar with a lid, scraping the bowl clean.

5. Chill for 30 minutes in the fridge—the dried herbs need time to bloom. Shake well before using; it's good for a week refrigerated.

**Nutritional Facts (per 2 tbsp / 30 ml):**

- Calories: 70
- Fat: 6 g (Saturated: 1 g)
- Carbs: 2 g (Sugars: 1 g)
- Protein: 2 g
- Sodium: 160 mg

### 3. Blue Cheese Dip
**Yield:** 1 cup (240 ml)

**Prep Time:** 15 minutes

**Ingredients:**

- ½ cup (120 g) sour cream
- ¼ cup (60 g) mayonnaise
- ½ cup (60 g) crumbled blue cheese
- 1 tbsp (15 ml) white vinegar
- 1 tsp (5 g) garlic powder
- ¼ tsp (1 g) ground black pepper

**Instructions:**

1. Scoop the sour cream and mayonnaise into a medium bowl—use a spatula to keep it neat. Add the crumbled blue cheese—pick a strong one like Gorgonzola—and stir with a fork to mix it in roughly; some chunks should stay.
2. Pour in the white vinegar and sprinkle the garlic powder and black pepper over the top. Switch to a whisk and blend for about a minute—work gently so the cheese doesn't dissolve completely; you want texture, not a paste.
3. Scrape the sides with your spatula and give it another quick whisk—look for a thick, creamy dip with blue flecks

throughout. If it's too stiff, add a teaspoon of milk or water and stir again.

4. Taste it—too mild? More blue cheese or a pinch of pepper. Too sharp? A dab of mayo. Tweak until it's bold but balanced, then spoon into a jar with a lid.

5. Chill for an hour in the fridge—it gets better as it sits. Stir before serving; keeps for a week refrigerated.

**Nutritional Facts (per 2 tbsp / 30 ml):**

- Calories: 100
- Fat: 10 g (Saturated: 4 g)
- Carbs: 1 g (Sugars: 0 g)
- Protein: 2 g
- Sodium: 200 mg

## 4. Alfredo Sauce

**Yield:** 2 cups (480 ml)

**Prep Time:** 10 minutes

**Cook Time:** 15 minutes

**Ingredients:**

- 1 cup (240 ml) heavy cream
- ½ cup (113 g) unsalted butter
- 1 cup (100 g) grated Parmesan cheese
- 1 garlic clove (about 3 g), minced
- ½ tsp (2 g) salt
- ¼ tsp (1 g) ground black pepper

**Instructions:**

1. Pour the heavy cream into a medium saucepan and add the butter—cut it into chunks first so it melts faster. Set over medium-low heat and stir with a wooden spoon as the butter softens and blends into the cream—about 3-5 minutes; don't let it boil.
2. Peel and mince the garlic fine—add it to the pan once the butter's fully melted. Keep stirring for a minute until it smells nutty, then slowly sprinkle in the Parmesan cheese,

a handful at a time—stir constantly so it melts smooth, not clumpy.

3. Cook for 5-7 minutes, stirring steadily—the sauce will thicken as the cheese blends in. Add the salt and pepper, then keep stirring until it's velvety and coats the spoon—don't crank the heat; low and slow is key.

4. Taste—too thin? Cook a minute more. Too bland? More Parmesan or salt. If it's grainy, whisk briskly off the heat for 30 seconds. Pull it off the stove and let it cool in the pan for 5 minutes, stirring occasionally.

5. Pour into a jar with a funnel—scrape the pan clean—and use right away or refrigerate for up to 3 days. Reheat gently with a splash of cream if it thickens too much.

**Nutritional Facts (per ¼ cup / 60 ml):**

- Calories: 300
- Fat: 30 g (Saturated: 19 g)
- Carbs: 2 g (Sugars: 1 g)
- Protein: 6 g
- Sodium: 400 mg

## 5. Tahini Sauce

**Yield:** 1 cup (240 ml)

**Prep Time:** 10 minutes

**Ingredients:**

- ½ cup (120 g) tahini
- ¼ cup (60 ml) water
- 2 tbsp (30 ml) lemon juice
- 1 garlic clove (about 3 g), minced
- ½ tsp (2 g) salt
- ¼ tsp (1 g) ground cumin

**Instructions:**

1. Scoop the tahini into a medium bowl—stir it first if it's separated; you want the thick paste. Pour in the water and lemon juice—go slow; it'll seize up at first—and whisk with a fork or small whisk for 30 seconds until it starts to smooth out.
2. Peel and mince the garlic fine—add it to the bowl with the salt and cumin. Whisk again, harder this time, for a full minute—work through the stiffness; it'll turn creamy as the water blends in. Scrape the sides with a spatula to keep it even.

3. Check the texture—too thick? Add a tablespoon more water and whisk until it's pourable but still rich. Too thin? A dollop of tahini. Keep going until it's silky and holds soft peaks.

4. Taste—more zing? Extra lemon. More depth? A pinch of cumin. Whisk after each tweak, then spoon into a jar with a tight lid—get every bit with your spatula.

5. Let it sit for 10 minutes at room temp to settle, then refrigerate for up to a week—stir before using if it separates.

**Nutritional Facts (per 2 tbsp / 30 ml):**

- Calories: 90
- Fat: 8 g (Saturated: 1 g)
- Carbs: 3 g (Sugars: 0 g)
- Protein: 3 g
- Sodium: 150 mg

## 6. Spicy Avocado Crema

**Yield:** 1.5 cups (360 ml)

**Prep Time:** 15 minutes

**Ingredients:**

- 2 ripe avocados (about 12 oz / 340 g), pitted
- ½ cup (120 g) sour cream
- 2 tbsp (30 ml) lime juice
- 1 jalapeño (about 1 oz / 28 g), seeded and minced
- ½ tsp (2 g) salt
- ¼ tsp (1 g) ground cumin

**Instructions:**

1. Slice the avocados in half, remove the pits, and scoop the flesh into a blender or food processor—use a spoon to get it all. Add the sour cream and lime juice right on top.
2. Rinse the jalapeño, slice it open, scrape out the seeds (leave 'em for heat), and mince it fine—add it to the mix with the salt and cumin. Blend on medium for 30 seconds—stop and scrape the sides with a spatula, then blend again for 15-20 seconds until it's smooth and creamy.

3. Check the consistency—too thick? Add a tablespoon of water and pulse again. Too runny? Another half avocado if you've got it. Scrape into a bowl and stir with a spoon to make sure it's even.
4. Taste—more kick? Extra jalapeño. More tang? A squeeze of lime. Adjust and blend briefly if needed, then spoon into a jar with a lid—press plastic wrap on the surface if you're not using it soon to keep it green.
5. Chill for 20 minutes in the fridge to set—stir before serving. Keeps for 3 days refrigerated.

**Nutritional Facts (per 2 tbsp / 30 ml):**

- Calories: 60
- Fat: 5 g (Saturated: 1 g)
- Carbs: 3 g (Sugars: 0 g)
- Protein: 1 g
- Sodium: 100 mg

## 7. Creamy Horseradish Sauce

**Yield:** 1 cup (240 ml)

**Prep Time:** 15 minutes

### Ingredients:

- ½ cup (120 g) sour cream
- ¼ cup (60 g) mayonnaise
- 2 tbsp (30 g) prepared horseradish
- 1 tbsp (15 ml) white vinegar
- ½ tsp (2 g) salt
- ¼ tsp (1 g) ground black pepper

### Instructions:

1. Measure the sour cream and mayonnaise into a medium bowl—scoop carefully with a spatula. Add the prepared horseradish—drain it if it's wet—and pour in the white vinegar.
2. Sprinkle the salt and black pepper over the top, then grab a whisk—stir gently at first with a spoon to mix the horseradish, then whisk briskly for a minute until it's smooth and creamy—no streaks or clumps.

3. Scrape the sides with your spatula and whisk again—look for a thick, spoonable sauce that holds its shape. If it's too stiff, add a teaspoon of water or vinegar and mix well.

4. Taste—too mild? More horseradish, a teaspoon at a time. Too sharp? A dab of sour cream. Tweak until it's bold but not overpowering, then transfer to a jar with a lid.

5. Chill for 30 minutes in the fridge—the bite mellows as it sits. Stir before serving; keeps for a week refrigerated.

**Nutritional Facts (per 2 tbsp / 30 ml):**

- Calories: 80
- Fat: 8 g (Saturated: 2 g)
- Carbs: 1 g (Sugars: 0 g)
- Protein: 1 g
- Sodium: 200 mg

## 8. Garlic Herb Cream Sauce

**Yield:** 1.5 cups (360 ml)

**Prep Time:** 15 minutes

**Cook Time:** 15 minutes

**Ingredients:**

- 1 cup (240 ml) heavy cream
- ¼ cup (60 g) cream cheese
- 2 garlic cloves (about 6 g), minced
- 1 tbsp (5 g) chopped fresh thyme
- 1 tbsp (5 g) chopped fresh parsley
- ½ tsp (2 g) salt
- ¼ tsp (1 g) ground black pepper

**Instructions:**

1. Pour the heavy cream into a medium saucepan and add the cream cheese—break it into chunks with your fingers. Set over medium-low heat and stir with a wooden spoon as it warms—about 3-5 minutes—until the cheese melts into the cream; keep stirring so it doesn't stick.
2. Peel and mince the garlic fine—add it to the pan once the mixture's smooth. Rinse the thyme and parsley, chop

them fine, and toss them in with the salt and pepper. Stir well for a minute—the garlic will soften and smell fragrant.

3. Cook for 10 minutes, stirring every couple minutes—the sauce will thicken slightly and bubble gently. Don't let it boil hard; lower the heat if it gets too hot. Scrape the sides to keep it even.
4. Taste—too thin? Cook 2-3 minutes more. Too bland? More herbs or salt. If it's lumpy, whisk off the heat for 30 seconds. Cool in the pan for 5 minutes, stirring occasionally, then pour into a jar with a funnel.
5. Refrigerate for up to 5 days—reheat gently with a splash of cream if needed. Serve warm.

**Nutritional Facts (per ¼ cup / 60 ml):**

- Calories: 200
- Fat: 20 g (Saturated: 12 g)
- Carbs: 2 g (Sugars: 1 g)
- Protein: 2 g
- Sodium: 250 mg

## 9. Cheddar Cheese Sauce

**Yield:** 2 cups (480 ml)

**Prep Time:** 10 minutes

**Cook Time:** 15 minutes

**Ingredients:**

- 2 tbsp (28 g) unsalted butter
- 2 tbsp (16 g) all-purpose flour
- 1 cup (240 ml) whole milk
- 1 cup (120 g) shredded sharp cheddar cheese
- ½ tsp (2 g) salt
- ¼ tsp (1 g) ground mustard powder

**Instructions:**

1. Melt the butter in a medium saucepan over medium heat—swirl it around until it's fully liquid, about 1-2 minutes. Sprinkle in the flour and whisk constantly for 1-2 minutes—it'll bubble and turn pale gold; don't let it brown.
2. Slowly pour in the milk, whisking nonstop—start with a trickle, then a steady stream. Keep going for 3-5 minutes as it thickens into a smooth base—no lumps; whisk harder if they form.

3. Lower the heat to medium-low and add the shredded cheddar a handful at a time—stir with a wooden spoon after each addition until it melts completely, about 5 minutes total. Add the salt and mustard powder with the last handful.
4. Cook for 2-3 minutes more, stirring steadily—the sauce should be thick and velvety, coating the spoon. Taste—more cheese for richness, or salt if it's flat. If it's grainy, whisk off the heat for 30 seconds.
5. Cool in the pan for 5 minutes, stirring occasionally, then pour into a jar with a funnel. Refrigerate for up to 5 days—reheat slowly with a splash of milk.

**Nutritional Facts (per ¼ cup / 60 ml):**

- Calories: 150
- Fat: 12 g (Saturated: 7 g)
- Carbs: 4 g (Sugars: 2 g)
- Protein: 6 g
- Sodium: 300 mg

## 10. Lemon Dill Cream

**Yield:** 1 cup (240 ml)

**Prep Time:** 15 minutes

**Ingredients:**

- ½ cup (120 g) sour cream
- ¼ cup (60 g) cream cheese
- 2 tbsp (30 ml) lemon juice
- 1 tbsp (5 g) chopped fresh dill
- 1 tsp (5 g) lemon zest
- ½ tsp (2 g) salt

**Instructions:**

1. Scoop the sour cream and cream cheese into a medium bowl—soften the cream cheese at room temp first if it's cold. Pour in the lemon juice and stir with a whisk for 30 seconds—it'll loosen up into a smooth mix.
2. Rinse the dill, pat dry, and chop it fine—add it to the bowl. Zest the lemon with a microplane—watch your fingers—and sprinkle in with the salt. Whisk again for a minute—work it until the herbs and zest are evenly flecked throughout.

3. Scrape the sides with a spatula and whisk once more—look for a thick, creamy sauce that holds soft peaks. If it's too stiff, add a teaspoon of water or lemon juice and mix again.
4. Taste—more brightness? Extra lemon juice or zest. Too tangy? A dab of sour cream. Adjust and whisk, then spoon into a jar with a lid—scrape it clean.
5. Chill for 30 minutes in the fridge to set—the dill will bloom. Stir before serving; keeps for a week refrigerated.

**Nutritional Facts (per 2 tbsp / 30 ml):**

- Calories: 60
- Fat: 5 g (Saturated: 3 g)
- Carbs: 1 g (Sugars: 0 g)
- Protein: 1 g
- Sodium: 150 mg

# Chapter 5: Pickled & Fermented Favorites

There's a magic in watching time turn simple ingredients into something tangy and alive—pickling and fermenting are like slow dances with flavor. I got hooked on sauerkraut back in my Navy days, stuck on a ship with a German cook named Hans who'd sneak jars of it from his bunk. One night, he caught me eyeing his stash and handed me a forkful—crisp, sour, and packed with punch. "Takes patience, kid," he said, showing me how he'd layered cabbage and salt in a cracked old crock. That taste stayed with me, and now I'm passing it on. This chapter's got ten recipes that bubble and brine their way to greatness—some quick, some slow, all worth the wait.

## 1. Sweet Pickle Relish

**Yield:** 2 cups (480 ml)

**Prep Time:** 20 minutes

**Cook Time:** 15 minutes

**Ingredients:**

- 2 cups (300 g) finely chopped cucumbers
- ½ cup (75 g) finely chopped onion
- ½ cup (120 ml) white vinegar
- ¼ cup (50 g) sugar
- 1 tsp (5 g) salt
- ½ tsp (2 g) mustard seeds
- ¼ tsp (1 g) celery seeds

**Instructions:**

1. Rinse the cucumbers under cold water, pat dry, and chop them fine—about ¼-inch pieces—on a cutting board; no big chunks. Peel and finely chop the onion too—keep it small so it blends in. Measure both into a medium saucepan.
2. Pour in the white vinegar, then add the sugar, salt, mustard seeds, and celery seeds. Set over medium-high

heat and stir with a wooden spoon—keep going for 3-5 minutes until the sugar dissolves and the mix starts to bubble; you'll smell the vinegar kick in.

3. Once it's boiling, drop the heat to medium-low for a gentle simmer—small bubbles should ripple through. Cook for 10-15 minutes, stirring every few minutes; the liquid will reduce, and the veggies will soften but hold their shape—scrape the bottom to avoid sticking.

4. After 10 minutes, check it—too wet? Simmer 2-3 more minutes until it's thick and spoonable. Taste—too tart? Add a teaspoon of sugar. Too mild? A pinch of salt. Stir well after adjusting to even it out.

5. Pull it off the heat and let it cool in the pan for 10-15 minutes—stir occasionally as it settles. Spoon into sterilized jars with a funnel, pressing down lightly to pack it in. Seal and refrigerate—it's good for 2 months.

**Nutritional Facts (per 1 tbsp / 15 ml):**

- Calories: 10
- Fat: 0 g
- Carbs: 2 g (Sugars: 2 g)
- Protein: 0 g
- Sodium: 75 mg

## 2. Sauerkraut

**Yield:** 4 cups (960 ml)

**Prep Time:** 30 minutes

**Fermentation Time:** 2-4 weeks

**Ingredients:**

- 2 lbs (900 g) green cabbage, shredded
- 1 tbsp (15 g) sea salt
- 1 tsp (5 g) caraway seeds (optional)

**Instructions:**

1. Peel off the cabbage's outer leaves—save one—and rinse the head. Quarter it, cut out the core, and shred fine with a sharp knife or mandoline—aim for ⅛-inch strands. Toss into a large mixing bowl.
2. Sprinkle the sea salt and caraway seeds (if using) over the cabbage. Massage it with clean hands—squeeze and knead for 5-10 minutes until it's juicy and limp; liquid will pool at the bottom. Keep going until it's wet enough to drip when you squeeze a handful.
3. Pack the cabbage into a clean quart jar—press down hard with your fist or a wooden spoon after each handful to

remove air pockets. Pour any leftover brine from the bowl over the top—cabbage should be submerged. Tuck the saved cabbage leaf on top as a cover.

4.  Weigh it down with a clean glass weight or a zip-top bag filled with water—keep everything under the brine. Cover the jar with a cloth, secure with a rubber band, and set in a cool, dark spot—check daily, pressing down if cabbage floats, for 2-4 weeks. Taste after 2 weeks—tangy and crisp? It's ready. Longer for more sourness.

5.  When it's to your liking, remove the weight and leaf, seal with a lid, and refrigerate—it'll keep for months. Stir before serving if brine settles.

**Nutritional Facts (per ¼ cup / 60 ml):**

- Calories: 15
- Fat: 0 g
- Carbs: 3 g (Sugars: 2 g)
- Protein: 1 g
- Sodium: 400 mg

## 3. Kimchi Paste

**Yield:** 1 cup (240 ml)

**Prep Time:** 20 minutes

**Fermentation Time:** 3-5 days

**Ingredients:**

- ½ cup (60 g) gochugaru (Korean red pepper flakes)
- ¼ cup (60 ml) fish sauce
- 2 tbsp (25 g) sugar
- 3 garlic cloves (about 9 g), minced
- 1 tbsp (15 g) minced fresh ginger
- 2 tbsp (30 ml) water

**Instructions:**

1. Measure the gochugaru into a medium bowl—watch the dust; it's potent. Pour in the fish sauce and water, then add the sugar—stir with a wooden spoon until it's a thick, wet paste; the sugar will start to dissolve.
2. Peel and mince the garlic and ginger fine—use a microplane if you've got one—and add them to the mix. Stir again for a minute—work it hard to blend the flavors; it'll smell sharp and spicy.

3. Scrape the paste into a clean jar—pack it down with your spoon to remove air bubbles; leave an inch of headspace. Seal loosely with a lid or cover with a cloth secured by a rubber band—fermentation needs a little air.

4. Set in a cool, dark spot for 3-5 days—check daily; it'll bubble and smell funkier each day. Stir once a day with a clean spoon to keep it even. Taste after 3 days—tangy and bold? It's good. Let it go longer for more depth.

5. When ready, tighten the lid and refrigerate—it's good for months. Stir before using as a condiment or rub.

**Nutritional Facts (per 1 tbsp / 15 ml):**

- Calories: 15
- Fat: 0 g
- Carbs: 3 g (Sugars: 2 g)
- Protein: 1 g
- Sodium: 300 mg

## 4. Pickled Jalapeños

**Yield:** 2 cups (480 ml)

**Prep Time:** 15 minutes

**Cook Time:** 10 minutes

**Ingredients:**

- 1 lb (450 g) jalapeños, sliced
- 1 cup (240 ml) white vinegar
- 1 cup (240 ml) water
- 2 tbsp (25 g) sugar
- 1 tbsp (15 g) salt
- 2 garlic cloves (about 6 g), peeled

**Instructions:**

1. Rinse the jalapeños, pat dry, and slice into ¼-inch rings—seeds in for heat, out for milder—on a cutting board. Pack them into a clean quart jar with the peeled garlic cloves—stuff 'em tight but leave an inch at the top.
2. Pour the white vinegar and water into a small saucepan, then add the sugar and salt. Set over medium-high heat and stir with a wooden spoon—keep going for 2-3 minutes until the sugar and salt dissolve completely; it'll look clear.

3. Bring to a boil—bubbles will roll hard—then pour the hot brine over the jalapeños in the jar; use a funnel to keep it neat. Tap the jar gently on the counter to release air bubbles—peppers should be submerged.
4. Let it cool to room temp—about 30 minutes—then taste a slice—too sweet? Next time less sugar. Too mild? More jalapeños. Seal with a lid and refrigerate—it's ready in an hour but best after a day. Keeps for 2 months.
5. Check the brine level after cooling—if it's low, top off with a mix of equal parts vinegar and water. Shake before serving.

**Nutritional Facts (per 2 tbsp / 30 ml):**

- Calories: 10
- Fat: 0 g
- Carbs: 2 g (Sugars: 1 g)
- Protein: 0 g
- Sodium: 200 mg

## 5. Fermented Garlic Honey

**Yield:** 1 cup (240 ml)

**Prep Time:** 15 minutes

**Fermentation Time:** 2-4 weeks

**Ingredients:**

- 1 cup (240 ml) raw honey
- 10 garlic cloves (about 30 g), peeled

**Instructions:**

1. Peel the garlic cloves—smash 'em lightly with the flat of a knife to slip the skins off—and rinse if they're dirty. Pat dry and pack into a clean pint jar—leave an inch of headspace.
2. Pour the raw honey over the garlic—go slow; it's thick—until they're fully covered; use a chopstick or skewer to poke out air bubbles. The honey will settle, so top off if needed to keep garlic submerged.
3. Seal loosely with a lid or cover with a cloth secured by a rubber band—fermentation needs air. Sct in a cool, dark spot—check daily for 2-4 weeks; flip the jar upside down

every day to mix it. Bubbles will form after a week; that's good.

4. Taste after 2 weeks—dip a clean spoon in; it'll be garlicky and slightly tangy. Want more funk? Let it go longer—up to 4 weeks. When it's ready, tighten the lid and refrigerate—it's good for months.

5. If it's too thick to pour, warm gently in a bowl of hot water—don't cook it. Stir before using.

**Nutritional Facts (per 1 tbsp / 15 ml):**

- Calories: 65
- Fat: 0 g
- Carbs: 17 g (Sugars: 16 g)
- Protein: 0 g
- Sodium: 0 mg

## 6. Quick Pickled Red Onions

**Yield:** 2 cups (480 ml)

**Prep Time:** 15 minutes

**Cook Time:** 5 minutes

**Ingredients:**

- 1 large red onion (about 12 oz / 340 g), thinly sliced
- ¾ cup (180 ml) apple cider vinegar
- ½ cup (120 ml) water
- 2 tbsp (25 g) sugar
- 1 tsp (5 g) salt

**Instructions:**

1. Peel the red onion and slice it thin—⅛-inch rings with a sharp knife or mandoline. Pack into a clean quart jar—stuff 'em in but leave room for brine.
2. Pour the apple cider vinegar and water into a small saucepan, then add the sugar and salt. Set over medium-high heat and stir with a wooden spoon—keep stirring for 2-3 minutes until it's clear and just boiling.

3. Pour the hot brine over the onions—use a funnel to avoid spills—until they're submerged; tap the jar on the counter to settle it. If any float, press down with a clean spoon.
4. Let it cool to room temp—about 30 minutes—then taste—too sweet? Less sugar next time. Too sharp? More water. Seal with a lid and refrigerate—it's ready in an hour, best after a day. Keeps for a month.
5. Shake the jar after cooling to mix the brine—top off with equal parts vinegar and water if needed.

**Nutritional Facts (per 2 tbsp / 30 ml):**

- Calories: 15
- Fat: 0 g
- Carbs: 3 g (Sugars: 2 g)
- Protein: 0 g
- Sodium: 150 mg

## 7. Fermented Carrot Sticks

**Yield:** 2 cups (480 ml)

**Prep Time:** 20 minutes

**Fermentation Time:** 1-2 weeks

**Ingredients:**

- 1 lb (450 g) carrots, peeled and cut into sticks
- 2 cups (480 ml) water
- 1 tbsp (15 g) sea salt
- 1 garlic clove (about 3 g), peeled
- 1 tsp (5 g) dill seeds

**Instructions:**

1. Peel the carrots and cut into 4-inch sticks—about ½-inch thick. Pack them upright into a clean quart jar with the peeled garlic clove and dill seeds—fit 'em snug but leave an inch at the top.
2. Mix the water and sea salt in a measuring cup—stir with a spoon until dissolved; this is your brine. Pour it over the carrots until they're submerged—tap the jar to release bubbles; they should stay under.

3. Weigh down with a clean glass weight or a zip-top bag filled with water—cover with a cloth and secure with a rubber band. Set in a cool, dark spot—check daily, pressing down if carrots float, for 1-2 weeks.
4. Taste after a week—crisp and tangy? It's done. Longer for more sourness—up to 2 weeks. When ready, remove the weight, seal with a lid, and refrigerate—it's good for months.
5. If brine clouds up (normal), skim any scum off the top—stir before serving.

**Nutritional Facts (per ¼ cup / 60 ml):**

- Calories: 20
- Fat: 0 g
- Carbs: 5 g (Sugars: 2 g)
- Protein: 0 g
- Sodium: 400 mg

## 8. Pickled Beets

**Yield:** 2 cups (480 ml)

**Prep Time:** 20 minutes

**Cook Time:** 30 minutes

**Ingredients:**

- 1 lb (450 g) beets, peeled and sliced
- 1 cup (240 ml) apple cider vinegar
- ½ cup (120 ml) water
- ¼ cup (50 g) sugar
- 1 tsp (5 g) salt
- ½ tsp (2 g) whole cloves

**Instructions:**

1. Rinse the beets, peel with a vegetable peeler, and slice into ¼-inch rounds—work on a cutting board; they'll stain. Pack into a clean quart jar—layer 'em tight but leave an inch at the top.
2. Pour the apple cider vinegar and water into a small saucepan, then add the sugar, salt, and whole cloves. Set over medium-high heat and stir with a wooden

spoon—keep going for 3-5 minutes until it's boiling and clear.

3. Pour the hot brine over the beets—use a funnel—until submerged; tap the jar to settle it. Let it cool to room temp—about 30-40 minutes—then taste a slice—too sweet? Less sugar next time. Too mild? More cloves.

4. Seal with a lid and refrigerate—it's ready in 24 hours but best after a few days. Keeps for a month—shake occasionally to mix the brine.

5. If beets float after cooling, press down with a clean spoon—top off with equal parts vinegar and water if needed.

**Nutritional Facts (per ¼ cup / 60 ml):**

- Calories: 40
- Fat: 0 g
- Carbs: 9 g (Sugars: 8 g)
- Protein: 1 g
- Sodium: 200 mg

## 9. Fermented Radish Slices

**Yield:** 2 cups (480 ml)

**Prep Time:** 20 minutes

**Fermentation Time:** 1-2 weeks

**Ingredients:**

- 1 lb (450 g) radishes, thinly sliced
- 2 cups (480 ml) water
- 1 tbsp (15 g) sea salt
- 1 tsp (5 g) black peppercorns
- 1 garlic clove (about 3 g), peeled

**Instructions:**

1. Rinse the radishes, trim the ends, and slice thin—⅛-inch rounds with a sharp knife or mandoline. Pack into a clean quart jar with the peeled garlic and peppercorns—layer 'em snug but leave an inch at the top.
2. Mix the water and sea salt in a measuring cup—stir until dissolved; this is your brine. Pour over the radishes until submerged—tap the jar to release bubbles; they need to stay under.

3. Weigh down with a clean glass weight or a zip-top bag filled with water—cover with a cloth and secure with a rubber band. Set in a cool, dark spot—check daily, pressing down if radishes float, for 1-2 weeks.

4. Taste after a week—crisp and tangy? It's good. Longer for more sourness—up to 2 weeks. When ready, remove the weight, seal with a lid, and refrigerate—it's good for months.

5. Skim any scum if it forms—stir before serving if brine settles.

**Nutritional Facts (per ¼ cup / 60 ml):**

- Calories: 10
- Fat: 0 g
- Carbs: 2 g (Sugars: 1 g)
- Protein: 0 g
- Sodium: 400 mg

## 10. Pickled Ginger

**Yield:** 1 cup (240 ml)

**Prep Time:** 15 minutes

**Cook Time:** 10 minutes

**Ingredients:**

- 8 oz (225 g) fresh ginger, peeled and thinly sliced
- ½ cup (120 ml) rice vinegar
- ¼ cup (50 g) sugar
- ½ tsp (2 g) salt
- ¼ cup (60 ml) water

**Instructions:**

1. Peel the ginger with a spoon—scrape the skin off—and slice thin—⅛-inch rounds with a sharp knife or mandoline. Pack into a clean pint jar—fit 'em tight but leave room for brine.
2. Pour the rice vinegar and water into a small saucepan, then add the sugar and salt. Set over medium-high heat and stir with a wooden spoon—keep going for 2-3 minutes until it's boiling and clear; the sugar will dissolve fast.

3. Pour the hot brine over the ginger—use a funnel—until submerged; tap the jar to settle it. Let it cool to room temp—about 20-30 minutes—then taste a slice—too sweet? Less sugar next time. Too sharp? More water.
4. Seal with a lid and refrigerate—it's ready in an hour but best after a day. Keeps for a month—shake occasionally to mix the brine.
5. If ginger floats after cooling, press down with a clean spoon—top off with equal parts vinegar and water if needed.

**Nutritional Facts (per 1 tbsp / 15 ml):**

- Calories: 20
- Fat: 0 g
- Carbs: 5 g (Sugars: 4 g)
- Protein: 0 g
- Sodium: 75 mg

## Chapter 6: Bold & Spicy

Heat's got a way of waking you up, and I learned that lesson hard in the Navy, halfway across the world in Jamaica. A cook named Marley handed me a bottle of his Scotch bonnet pepper sauce—bright orange and innocent-looking—during a shore leave barbecue. I splashed it on some jerk chicken, took a bite, and felt my whole head light up like a flare. Sweat, tears, and a grin I couldn't shake—he laughed and said, "That's the island talking, mon." I've been chasing that fire ever since. This chapter's for the heat lovers—ten recipes that pack a punch, from sneaky to downright fierce. Grab a glass of milk and let's get bold.

## 1. Gochujang (Korea)

**Yield:** 2 cups (480 ml)

**Prep Time:** 30 minutes

**Fermentation Time:** 2 weeks

**Ingredients:**

- 1 cup (120 g) gochugaru (Korean red pepper flakes)
- ½ cup (100 g) sweet rice flour
- ¼ cup (50 g) sugar
- ¼ cup (60 ml) soy sauce
- 2 tbsp (30 g) salt
- 2 cups (480 ml) water

**Instructions:**

1. Measure the sweet rice flour into a medium saucepan and pour in the water—whisk with a fork until it's lump-free; you want a smooth slurry. Set over medium heat and stir constantly with a wooden spoon—about 5-7 minutes—until it thickens into a sticky paste; it'll look like glue when it's ready. Cool it in the pan for 15 minutes until it's just warm.

2. Once cooled, stir in the gochugaru—add it gradually so it doesn't clump—then mix in the sugar, soy sauce, and salt. Use your spoon to blend it into a vibrant red paste—stir hard for a minute to wake up the spices; it'll feel gritty but cohesive.

3. Scrape the mixture into a wide, shallow glass container—more surface area speeds fermentation. Press it down with your spoon to remove air pockets, then cover with a clean cloth and secure with a rubber band—don't seal it tight; it needs to breathe.

4. Set in a cool, dark spot—check daily for 2 weeks. Stir once a day with a clean spoon—look for bubbles after a few days; it'll smell spicy-sweet and tangy by week one. Taste after 10 days—bold and complex? It's ready. Let it go longer for deeper funk, up to 2 weeks.

5. When it's to your liking, spoon into a jar—pack it tight—and seal with a lid. Refrigerate—it's good for months. Stir well before using; it settles over time.

**Nutritional Facts (per 1 tbsp / 15 ml):**

- Calories: 20
- Fat: 0 g
- Carbs: 4 g (Sugars: 2 g)
- Protein: 1 g

- Sodium: 300 mg

## 2. Scotch Bonnet Pepper Sauce (Caribbean)

**Yield:** 1 cup (240 ml)

**Prep Time:** 20 minutes

**Cook Time:** 15 minutes

### Ingredients:

- 10 Scotch bonnet peppers (about 2 oz / 56 g), stemmed
- 1 small mango (about 6 oz / 170 g), peeled and chopped
- ½ cup (120 ml) white vinegar
- 2 garlic cloves (about 6 g), peeled
- 1 tbsp (12 g) sugar
- ½ tsp (2 g) salt

### Instructions:

1. Rinse the Scotch bonnets—wear gloves if you're smart—and slice off the stems; leave seeds for max heat, remove some for less. Peel and chop the mango into 1-inch chunks—discard the pit. Toss both into a blender with the peeled garlic.
2. Pour in the white vinegar, then add the sugar and salt. Blend on high for 1-2 minutes—stop and scrape the sides

with a spatula if it sticks—until it's a smooth, fiery orange puree; watch the fumes, they'll sting.

3. Pour the puree into a small saucepan and set over medium heat. Bring to a simmer—stir with a wooden spoon as it bubbles, about 3-5 minutes—then lower to medium-low. Cook for 10 minutes, stirring every couple minutes; it'll thicken slightly and darken a shade.

4. Taste a tiny bit—too hot? Add a teaspoon of sugar. Too tart? More mango next time. Cool in the pan for 10 minutes—stir occasionally—then pour into a jar with a funnel; strain through a fine mesh sieve if you want it smoother.

5. Seal and refrigerate—it's ready in an hour but better after a day. Keeps for a month—shake before using; it might separate.

**Nutritional Facts (per 1 tbsp / 15 ml):**

- Calories: 15
- Fat: 0 g
- Carbs: 3 g (Sugars: 2 g)
- Protein: 0 g
- Sodium: 75 mg

### 3. Chipotle Adobo Sauce

**Yield:** 1.5 cups (360 ml)

**Prep Time:** 20 minutes

**Cook Time:** 25 minutes

**Ingredients:**

- 6 dried chipotle peppers (about 2 oz / 56 g), stemmed
- 1 cup (240 ml) tomato puree
- ½ cup (120 ml) water
- ¼ cup (60 ml) apple cider vinegar
- 2 tbsp (25 g) brown sugar
- 2 garlic cloves (about 6 g), peeled
- ½ tsp (2 g) salt

**Instructions:**

1. Rinse the chipotles and snip off the stems with scissors—soak in hot water for 15 minutes to soften; drain and pat dry. Toss into a blender with the tomato puree, water, apple cider vinegar, brown sugar, peeled garlic, and salt.
2. Blend on high for 1-2 minutes—scrape the sides with a spatula—until it's a smooth, smoky red paste; seeds will

speckle it, that's fine. Pour into a medium saucepan and set over medium heat.

3. Bring to a simmer—stir with a wooden spoon as it bubbles, about 5 minutes—then drop to low. Cook for 20 minutes, stirring every 5 minutes; it'll thicken and darken, coating the spoon—watch it close; it can stick if you're not careful.

4. Taste—too mild? Add a pinch of chili powder. Too sweet? A splash of vinegar. Cool in the pan for 10 minutes—stir occasionally—then spoon into a jar with a funnel; strain if you want it silkier.

5. Seal and refrigerate—it's good for a month. Stir before using; it settles.

**Nutritional Facts (per 2 tbsp / 30 ml):**

- Calories: 25
- Fat: 0 g
- Carbs: 6 g (Sugars: 4 g)
- Protein: 1 g
- Sodium: 150 mg

## 4. Peri-Peri Sauce (South Africa)

**Yield:** 1 cup (240 ml)

**Prep Time:** 20 minutes

**Cook Time:** 15 minutes

**Ingredients:**

- 10 bird's eye chilies (about 2 oz / 56 g), stemmed
- 1 red bell pepper (about 6 oz / 170 g), chopped
- 3 garlic cloves (about 9 g), peeled
- ¼ cup (60 ml) olive oil
- 2 tbsp (30 ml) lemon juice
- 1 tsp (5 g) smoked paprika
- ½ tsp (2 g) salt

**Instructions:**

1. Rinse the bird's eye chilies—stem 'em but keep seeds for fire—and chop the red bell pepper into 1-inch chunks; toss both into a blender with the peeled garlic. Pour in the olive oil and lemon juice, then add the smoked paprika and salt.
2. Blend on high for 1-2 minutes—scrape the sides with a spatula—until it's a smooth, bright orange-red sauce; no

big chunks left. Pour into a small saucepan and set over medium heat.

3. Bring to a simmer—stir with a wooden spoon as it bubbles, about 3-5 minutes—then lower to medium-low. Cook for 10 minutes, stirring every couple minutes; it'll thicken a bit and smell smoky-spicy—don't let it burn; keep the heat gentle.

4. Taste—too hot? Add a teaspoon of oil. Too tame? More chilies next time. Cool in the pan for 10 minutes—stir occasionally—then pour into a jar with a funnel; strain if you want it smoother.

5. Seal and refrigerate—it's good for a month. Shake before using; oil might separate.

**Nutritional Facts (per 1 tbsp / 15 ml):**

- Calories: 40
- Fat: 4 g (Saturated: 0.5 g)
- Carbs: 2 g (Sugars: 1 g)
- Protein: 0 g
- Sodium: 75 mg

## 5. Ghost Pepper Salsa

**Yield:** 1.5 cups (360 ml)

**Prep Time:** 20 minutes

**Cook Time:** 10 minutes

**Ingredients:**

- 1 lb (450 g) tomatoes, chopped
- 2 ghost peppers (about 0.5 oz / 14 g), stemmed
- ½ cup (75 g) chopped onion
- 2 garlic cloves (about 6 g), peeled
- 2 tbsp (30 ml) lime juice
- ½ tsp (2 g) salt

**Instructions:**

1. Rinse the tomatoes, chop into ½-inch pieces—discard tough cores—and toss into a blender. Rinse the ghost peppers—wear gloves; they're brutal—stem 'em, and add with the chopped onion and peeled garlic.
2. Pour in the lime juice and sprinkle the salt—blend on high for 1-2 minutes—scrape the sides with a spatula—until it's a chunky salsa; smooth's fine too, just blend longer. Pour into a small saucepan and set over medium heat.

3. Bring to a simmer—stir with a wooden spoon as it bubbles, about 3-5 minutes—then lower to medium-low. Cook for 5-7 minutes, stirring often; it'll thicken slightly—watch out; ghost peppers pack heat that builds.
4. Taste a tiny bit—too fiery? Add a teaspoon of sugar. Too mild? You're braver than me. Cool in the pan for 10 minutes—stir occasionally—then spoon into a jar with a funnel; strain if you want it less pulpy.
5. Seal and refrigerate—it's good for a month. Shake before using—warn your guests.

**Nutritional Facts (per 2 tbsp / 30 ml):**

- Calories: 15
- Fat: 0 g
- Carbs: 3 g (Sugars: 2 g)
- Protein: 1 g
- Sodium: 100 mg

## 6. Habanero Hot Sauce

**Yield:** 1 cup (240 ml)

**Prep Time:** 20 minutes

**Cook Time:** 15 minutes

### Ingredients:

- 10 habanero peppers (about 2 oz / 56 g), stemmed
- ½ cup (120 ml) white vinegar
- ¼ cup (60 ml) water
- 2 garlic cloves (about 6 g), peeled
- 1 tbsp (12 g) sugar
- ½ tsp (2 g) salt

### Instructions:

1. Rinse the habaneros—gloves on—and slice off the stems; seeds stay for heat. Toss into a blender with the white vinegar, water, peeled garlic, sugar, and salt—blend on high for 1-2 minutes—scrape the sides—until it's a smooth, orange firestorm.
2. Pour into a small saucepan and set over medium heat. Bring to a simmer—stir with a wooden spoon as it bubbles, about 3-5 minutes—then lower to medium-low.

Cook for 10 minutes, stirring every couple minutes; it'll thicken a touch and smell intense—ventilate your kitchen.

3. Taste a drop—too hot? More sugar. Too tart? Less vinegar next time. Cool in the pan for 10 minutes—stir occasionally—then pour into a jar with a funnel; strain if you want it sleek.

4. Seal and refrigerate—it's ready in an hour but better after a day. Keeps for a month—shake before using; it's a slow burn.

5. If it separates, give it a good shake—top off with vinegar if it looks low.

**Nutritional Facts (per 1 tsp / 5 ml):**

- Calories: 5
- Fat: 0 g
- Carbs: 1 g (Sugars: 1 g)
- Protein: 0 g
- Sodium: 50 mg

## 7. Szechuan Chili Oil

**Yield:** 1.5 cups (360 ml)

**Prep Time:** 15 minutes

**Cook Time:** 20 minutes

### Ingredients:

- 1 cup (240 ml) vegetable oil
- ¼ cup (30 g) crushed red pepper flakes
- 2 tbsp (15 g) Szechuan peppercorns
- 1 tbsp (15 g) sesame seeds
- 1 garlic clove (about 3 g), minced
- ½ tsp (2 g) salt

### Instructions:

1. Pour the vegetable oil into a small saucepan and add the crushed red pepper flakes, Szechuan peppercorns, sesame seeds, minced garlic, and salt—stir with a wooden spoon to mix it up.
2. Set over medium-low heat—go slow; you're infusing, not frying. Stir occasionally for 5-7 minutes until it starts to sizzle gently—watch the garlic; if it browns too fast, lower

the heat. Cook for 15 minutes total; the oil will turn red and smell nutty-spicy.

3. Pull it off the heat and let it cool in the pan for 10-15 minutes—stir now and then; the flavors keep steeping. Taste a drop—too mild? Add more flakes next time. Too strong? More oil.

4. Strain through a fine mesh sieve into a jar—press the solids with a spoon to get every drop; keep the crunchy bits if you like texture. Let it cool completely—about 30 minutes—then seal with a lid.

5. Refrigerate—it's good for a month. Shake before using; it settles.

**Nutritional Facts (per 1 tbsp / 15 ml):**

- Calories: 90
- Fat: 10 g (Saturated: 1 g)
- Carbs: 1 g (Sugars: 0 g)
- Protein: 0 g
- Sodium: 50 mg

## 8. Thai Chili Paste (Nam Prik Pao)

**Yield:** 1 cup (240 ml)

**Prep Time:** 20 minutes

**Cook Time:** 15 minutes

**Ingredients:**

- 10 dried red chilies (about 2 oz / 56 g), stemmed
- ¼ cup (60 ml) vegetable oil
- 2 garlic cloves (about 6 g), peeled
- 1 shallot (about 2 oz / 56 g), chopped
- 1 tbsp (15 g) tamarind paste
- 1 tbsp (12 g) brown sugar
- ½ tsp (2 g) salt

**Instructions:**

1. Soak the dried chilies in hot water for 15 minutes—drain and pat dry; snip off stems. Heat the vegetable oil in a small skillet over medium heat—add the chilies, garlic, and chopped shallot; fry for 5-7 minutes, stirring with a wooden spoon until they're fragrant and slightly crisp—don't burn 'em.

2. Scoop the fried mix into a blender—add the tamarind paste, brown sugar, and salt. Blend on high for 1-2 minutes—scrape the sides—until it's a thick, oily paste; add a tablespoon of water if it's too dry.
3. Pour back into the skillet and set over medium-low heat. Cook for 5-7 minutes—stir constantly; it'll darken and thicken into a jam-like paste—scrape the bottom to avoid sticking.
4. Taste—too sour? More sugar. Too mild? More chilies next time. Cool in the skillet for 10 minutes—stir occasionally—then spoon into a jar with a spatula; no straining here, keep the texture.
5. Seal and refrigerate—it's good for a month. Stir before using; it's sticky.

**Nutritional Facts (per 1 tbsp / 15 ml):**

- Calories: 50
- Fat: 4 g (Saturated: 0.5 g)
- Carbs: 3 g (Sugars: 2 g)
- Protein: 0 g
- Sodium: 75 mg

## 9. Harissa (North Africa)

**Yield:** 1 cup (240 ml)

**Prep Time:** 20 minutes

**Cook Time:** 10 minutes

**Ingredients:**

- 10 dried red chilies (about 2 oz / 56 g), stemmed and seeded
- 1 tsp (5 g) caraway seeds
- 1 tsp (5 g) coriander seeds
- ½ tsp (2 g) cumin seeds
- 3 garlic cloves (about 9 g), peeled
- ½ cup (120 ml) olive oil
- 1 tsp (5 g) salt

**Instructions:**

1. Soak the dried chilies in hot water for 15 minutes—drain and pat dry; chop roughly. Toast the caraway, coriander, and cumin seeds in a dry skillet over medium heat—shake for 2-3 minutes until fragrant—then grind in a spice grinder or mortar and pestle into a fine powder.

2. Toss the chilies, ground spices, peeled garlic, olive oil, and salt into a blender—blend on high for 1-2 minutes—scrape the sides—until it's a thick, grainy paste; smooth's okay too, just blend longer.
3. Pour into a small saucepan and set over low heat. Cook for 5-7 minutes—stir constantly with a wooden spoon; it'll deepen in color and smell smoky—don't let it burn; keep it gentle.
4. Taste—too mild? More chilies. Too dry? A splash of oil. Cool in the pan for 10 minutes—stir occasionally—then spoon into a jar; cover with a thin layer of olive oil to seal.
5. Refrigerate—it's good for a month. Stir before using; it settles.

**Nutritional Facts (per 1 tbsp / 15 ml):**

- Calories: 70
- Fat: 7 g (Saturated: 1 g)
- Carbs: 2 g (Sugars: 1 g)
- Protein: 0 g
- Sodium: 150 mg

## 10. Spicy Mango Chutney

**Yield:** 2 cups (480 ml)

**Prep Time:** 20 minutes

**Cook Time:** 30 minutes

**Ingredients:**

- 2 mangoes (about 1 lb / 450 g), peeled and chopped
- ½ cup (100 g) sugar
- ½ cup (120 ml) white vinegar
- 2 red chilies (about 1 oz / 28 g), finely chopped
- 1 tbsp (15 g) minced fresh ginger
- ½ tsp (2 g) salt
- ¼ tsp (1 g) ground cloves

**Instructions:**

1. Peel the mangoes—use a peeler or knife—and chop into ½-inch chunks; discard the pit. Toss into a medium saucepan with the sugar, white vinegar, and finely chopped red chilies—seeds in for heat.
2. Peel and mince the ginger fine—add it with the salt and ground cloves. Set over medium heat and stir with a

wooden spoon—keep going for 5 minutes until the sugar dissolves and the mango starts to juice up.

3. Bring to a simmer—bubbles will foam—then lower to medium-low. Cook for 25-30 minutes—stir every 5 minutes; the mango will soften into a thick, spicy jam—scrape the bottom to avoid sticking; it'll darken a bit.

4. Taste—too sweet? More vinegar. Too mild? More chilies next time. If it's too runny, cook 5 more minutes—watch close; it thickens fast. Cool in the pan for 15 minutes—stir occasionally—then spoon into jars with a funnel.

5. Seal and refrigerate—it's good for a month. Stir before serving; it's chunky.

**Nutritional Facts (per 2 tbsp / 30 ml):**

- Calories: 50
- Fat: 0 g
- Carbs: 12 g (Sugars: 11 g)
- Protein: 0 g
- Sodium: 75 mg

# Chapter 7: Finishing Touches

Sometimes a dish just needs a little nudge to shine, and that's where these quick sauces come in—they're the last brushstroke on the canvas. I learned that with lemon-garlic butter sauce one frantic night in Austin. My wife had friends over, the chicken was dry as a bone, and I was sweating bullets. I melted some butter, tossed in garlic and a squeeze of lemon, and drizzled it over everything—suddenly, they were raving like I'd planned it all along. That's the beauty of a finishing touch: fast, simple, and a total game-changer. This chapter's got ten recipes to drizzle, dip, or dollop—little heroes for when you need a meal to sing at the last second.

# 1. Herb-Infused Olive Oil

**Yield:** 1 cup (240 ml)

**Prep Time:** 10 minutes

**Cook Time:** 10 minutes

**Ingredients:**

- 1 cup (240 ml) olive oil
- 2 tbsp (10 g) fresh rosemary, chopped
- 2 tbsp (10 g) fresh thyme, chopped
- 1 garlic clove (about 3 g), peeled and smashed

**Instructions:**

1. Measure the olive oil into a small saucepan—use a good extra-virgin kind for flavor. Rinse the rosemary and thyme, pat dry with a towel, and chop them roughly—stems off, just leaves. Peel the garlic and smash it with the flat of a knife—add all three to the oil.
2. Set the pan over low heat—really low; you're infusing, not frying. Stir with a wooden spoon for a minute to mix it up, then let it warm for 8-10 minutes—watch for tiny bubbles around the herbs; if it smokes, pull it off quick.

3. After 10 minutes, the oil should smell herby and the garlic golden—don't let it brown too much; it'll bitter up. Pull it off the heat and cool in the pan for 15 minutes—stir once or twice as it settles; the flavors keep steeping.
4. Strain through a fine mesh sieve into a clean jar—press the herbs with a spoon to get every drop; discard the solids. Taste a dip—too mild? More herbs next time. Too strong? Cut the heat time.
5. Seal and store at room temp—it's good for a month. Shake before drizzling; it might settle.

**Nutritional Facts (per 1 tbsp / 15 ml):**

- Calories: 120
- Fat: 14 g (Saturated: 2 g)
- Carbs: 0 g
- Protein: 0 g
- Sodium: 0 mg

## 2. Lemon-Garlic Butter Sauce

**Yield:** ½ cup (120 ml)

**Prep Time:** 10 minutes

**Cook Time:** 5 minutes

**Ingredients:**

- ½ cup (113 g) unsalted butter
- 2 garlic cloves (about 6 g), minced
- 2 tbsp (30 ml) lemon juice
- ½ tsp (2 g) salt
- ¼ tsp (1 g) ground black pepper

**Instructions:**

1. Cut the butter into chunks and toss into a small saucepan—set over medium-low heat. Stir with a wooden spoon as it melts—takes about 2-3 minutes—until it's fully liquid and just starting to bubble; don't let it brown.
2. Peel and mince the garlic fine—add it to the butter and stir for 30 seconds; it'll sizzle and smell nutty. Pour in the lemon juice—watch for splatter—then add the salt and pepper. Stir briskly for a minute to blend it all; it'll foam a bit.

3. Cook for 1-2 minutes more—keep stirring; the sauce should thicken slightly and coat the spoon. If it separates, whisk hard off the heat for 30 seconds to bring it back—low heat's key here.
4. Taste—more zing? Extra lemon. Too bland? A pinch of salt. Pull it off the heat and cool in the pan for 5 minutes—stir occasionally—then pour into a jar with a funnel or serve warm right away.
5. Refrigerate if saving—it's good for a week. Reheat gently; it solidifies when cold.

**Nutritional Facts (per 1 tbsp / 15 ml):**

- Calories: 100
- Fat: 11 g (Saturated: 7 g)
- Carbs: 0 g
- Protein: 0 g
- Sodium: 150 mg

## 3. Truffle Aioli

**Yield:** 1 cup (240 ml)

**Prep Time:** 15 minutes

**Ingredients:**

- ¾ cup (180 g) mayonnaise
- 1 tbsp (15 ml) truffle oil
- 1 garlic clove (about 3 g), minced
- 1 tsp (5 ml) lemon juice
- ½ tsp (2 g) salt
- ¼ tsp (1 g) ground black pepper

**Instructions:**

1. Scoop the mayonnaise into a medium bowl—use a good one; it's the base. Pour in the truffle oil—go easy; it's strong—then peel and mince the garlic fine; add it with the lemon juice, salt, and pepper.
2. Stir with a whisk—start slow to mix the oil in, then whisk briskly for a minute; work from the center out until it's smooth and glossy—scrape the sides with a spatula to keep it even; no lumps or streaks.
3. Check the texture—too thick? Add a teaspoon of water and whisk again. Too thin? More mayo. It should hold soft

peaks and smell earthy from the truffle—don't overdo the oil; it'll overpower.

4. Taste—more depth? A drop of truffle oil. More bite? Extra lemon. Whisk after each tweak, then spoon into a jar with a tight lid—get every bit with your spatula.

5. Chill for 30 minutes in the fridge—the flavors meld better cold. Stir before serving; keeps for a week.

**Nutritional Facts (per 1 tbsp / 15 ml):**

- Calories: 90
- Fat: 10 g (Saturated: 1.5 g)
- Carbs: 0 g
- Protein: 0 g
- Sodium: 150 mg

## 4. Soy-Ginger Glaze

**Yield:** ½ cup (120 ml)

**Prep Time:** 10 minutes

**Cook Time:** 10 minutes

**Ingredients:**

- ¼ cup (60 ml) soy sauce
- 2 tbsp (30 ml) honey
- 1 tbsp (15 ml) rice vinegar
- 1 tbsp (15 g) minced fresh ginger
- 1 garlic clove (about 3 g), minced
- 1 tsp (5 ml) sesame oil

**Instructions:**

1. Pour the soy sauce into a small saucepan—add the honey and rice vinegar. Peel and mince the ginger and garlic fine—use a microplane if you've got one—and toss them in with the sesame oil.
2. Set over medium heat and stir with a wooden spoon—keep going for 2-3 minutes until the honey dissolves and it starts to bubble gently; you'll smell the ginger and garlic waking up.

3. Lower to medium-low and simmer for 5-7 minutes—stir every minute; it'll reduce and thicken into a sticky glaze—scrape the sides to keep it even; don't let it burn; it's quick to catch.
4. Taste—too salty? More honey. Too thin? Cook a minute more. Cool in the pan for 5 minutes—stir occasionally—then pour into a jar with a funnel; it'll firm up as it cools.
5. Refrigerate—it's good for a month. Warm gently if it gets too thick; drizzle warm.

**Nutritional Facts (per 1 tbsp / 15 ml):**

- Calories: 25
- Fat: 0.5 g (Saturated: 0 g)
- Carbs: 5 g (Sugars: 4 g)
- Protein: 1 g
- Sodium: 450 mg

## 5. Quick Pan Gravy (No Drippings)

**Yield:** 1 cup (240 ml)

**Prep Time:** 5 minutes

**Cook Time:** 10 minutes

**Ingredients:**

- 2 tbsp (28 g) unsalted butter
- 2 tbsp (16 g) all-purpose flour
- 1 cup (240 ml) chicken broth
- ½ tsp (2 g) salt
- ¼ tsp (1 g) ground black pepper
- 1 tsp (5 ml) Worcestershire sauce

**Instructions:**

1. Melt the butter in a small saucepan over medium heat—swirl it around until it's liquid, about 1-2 minutes. Sprinkle in the flour and whisk constantly—keep going for 1-2 minutes until it's a pale gold paste; don't let it brown; it's a roux.
2. Slowly pour in the chicken broth—start with a trickle, whisking nonstop, then a steady stream—takes 3-5

minutes to thicken into a smooth base; no lumps; whisk harder if they pop up.

3. Add the salt, pepper, and Worcestershire sauce—whisk for a minute to blend; it'll darken slightly and smell savory. Simmer for 3-5 minutes—stir with a wooden spoon now; it should coat the spoon lightly.

4. Taste—too thin? Cook a minute more. Too bland? More salt or a splash of broth. If it's lumpy, strain through a fine mesh sieve. Cool in the pan for 5 minutes—stir occasionally—then pour into a jar or serve warm.

5. Refrigerate—it's good for 3 days. Reheat with a splash of broth if it thickens.

**Nutritional Facts (per ¼ cup / 60 ml):**

- Calories: 70
- Fat: 6 g (Saturated: 4 g)
- Carbs: 4 g (Sugars: 0 g)
- Protein: 1 g
- Sodium: 400 mg

## 6. Spicy Honey Drizzle

**Yield:** ½ cup (120 ml)

**Prep Time:** 10 minutes

**Cook Time:** 5 minutes

**Ingredients:**

- ½ cup (120 ml) honey
- 1 tsp (5 g) red pepper flakes
- 1 tbsp (15 ml) apple cider vinegar
- ¼ tsp (1 g) salt

**Instructions:**

1. Measure the honey into a small saucepan—scrape the spoon clean; it's sticky. Add the red pepper flakes, apple cider vinegar, and salt—stir with a wooden spoon to mix it up.
2. Set over low heat—gentle now; you're warming, not boiling. Stir for 2-3 minutes until the honey thins and the flakes start to sizzle—don't let it bubble hard; it'll foam if you do.
3. Cook for 2 more minutes—stir constantly; it'll smell sweet-spicy and turn a shade darker. Pull it off the heat if

it gets too hot—taste a drop; too mild? More flakes. Too sharp? More honey.

4. Cool in the pan for 10 minutes—stir occasionally; it'll thicken as it cools. Strain through a fine mesh sieve into a jar if you want it smooth—keep the flakes if you like texture.

5. Seal and store at room temp—it's good for a month. Warm gently if it firms up; drizzle warm.

**Nutritional Facts (per 1 tbsp / 15 ml):**

- Calories: 65
- Fat: 0 g
- Carbs: 17 g (Sugars: 16 g)
- Protein: 0 g
- Sodium: 75 mg

## 7. Balsamic Reduction

**Yield:** ½ cup (120 ml)

**Prep Time:** 5 minutes

**Cook Time:** 15 minutes

**Ingredients:**

- 1 cup (240 ml) balsamic vinegar
- 2 tbsp (25 g) sugar

**Instructions:**

1. Pour the balsamic vinegar into a small saucepan—add the sugar and stir with a wooden spoon over medium heat—keep going for 2-3 minutes until the sugar dissolves; it'll look murky at first.
2. Bring to a simmer—small bubbles will form—then lower to medium-low. Cook for 10-15 minutes—stir every few minutes; it'll reduce by half and thicken into a syrup—scrape the sides; it sticks as it cooks.
3. Check after 10 minutes—too thin? Keep going; it should coat the spoon and hold a line when you drag a finger through. Too thick? Add a tablespoon of water and stir—don't overdo it; it firms up as it cools.

4. Taste—too tart? More sugar. Too sweet? Less next time. Cool in the pan for 5 minutes—stir occasionally—then pour into a jar with a funnel; it'll glossy up as it sits.
5. Refrigerate—it's good for a month. Drizzle cold or warm; it thickens when chilled.

**Nutritional Facts (per 1 tbsp / 15 ml):**

- Calories: 40
- Fat: 0 g
- Carbs: 9 g (Sugars: 8 g)
- Protein: 0 g
- Sodium: 5 mg

## 8. Garlic Chili Oil

**Yield:** 1 cup (240 ml)

**Prep Time:** 10 minutes

**Cook Time:** 15 minutes

**Ingredients:**

- 1 cup (240 ml) vegetable oil
- 2 tbsp (15 g) crushed red pepper flakes
- 3 garlic cloves (about 9 g), minced
- ½ tsp (2 g) salt

**Instructions:**

1. Pour the vegetable oil into a small saucepan—add the crushed red pepper flakes, minced garlic, and salt. Stir with a wooden spoon to mix it up—get the flakes evenly spread.
2. Set over low heat—slow is key; you're infusing. Stir occasionally for 5-7 minutes until it sizzles gently—watch the garlic; if it browns too fast, lower the heat. Cook for 10-15 minutes total; the oil will turn red and smell spicy-garlicky.

3. Pull it off the heat and cool in the pan for 15 minutes—stir now and then; the flavors keep deepening. Taste a drop—too mild? More flakes next time. Too strong? More oil.

4. Strain through a fine mesh sieve into a jar—press the solids to get every drop; keep 'em if you like crunch. Let it cool completely—about 30 minutes—then seal with a lid.

5. Refrigerate—it's good for a month. Shake before drizzling; it settles.

**Nutritional Facts (per 1 tbsp / 15 ml):**

- Calories: 120
- Fat: 14 g (Saturated: 1 g)
- Carbs: 0 g
- Protein: 0 g
- Sodium: 50 mg

## 9. Herbed Yogurt Sauce
**Yield:** 1 cup (240 ml)

**Prep Time:** 10 minutes

**Ingredients:**

- 1 cup (240 g) Greek yogurt
- 1 tbsp (5 g) chopped fresh mint
- 1 tbsp (5 g) chopped fresh dill
- 1 tsp (5 ml) lemon juice
- ½ tsp (2 g) salt
- ¼ tsp (1 g) ground black pepper

**Instructions:**

1. Scoop the Greek yogurt into a medium bowl—full-fat's best for creaminess. Rinse the mint and dill, pat dry, and chop them fine—no stems; just leaves—add to the yogurt with the lemon juice, salt, and pepper.
2. Stir with a whisk—start slow to mix the herbs, then whisk briskly for a minute; work it until it's smooth and flecked with green—scrape the sides with a spatula to keep it even; no clumps.
3. Check the texture—too thick? Add a teaspoon of water and whisk again. Too thin? More yogurt. It should be

creamy and spoonable—taste; more zing? Extra lemon. More kick? A pinch of pepper.

4. Whisk after each tweak, then spoon into a jar with a tight lid—get every bit with your spatula. Chill for 20 minutes in the fridge—the herbs bloom as it sits.

5. Stir before serving; keeps for a week refrigerated.

**Nutritional Facts (per 2 tbsp / 30 ml):**

- Calories: 30
- Fat: 1 g (Saturated: 0.5 g)
- Carbs: 2 g (Sugars: 1 g)
- Protein: 3 g
- Sodium: 150 mg

## 10. Maple Mustard Glaze

**Yield:** ½ cup (120 ml)

**Prep Time:** 10 minutes

### Ingredients:

- ¼ cup (60 ml) maple syrup
- 2 tbsp (30 g) Dijon mustard
- 1 tbsp (15 ml) apple cider vinegar
- ½ tsp (2 g) salt
- ¼ tsp (1 g) ground black pepper

### Instructions:

1. Measure the maple syrup into a small bowl—scrape the spoon clean; it's sticky. Add the Dijon mustard, apple cider vinegar, salt, and pepper—stir with a whisk to mix it up; start slow to blend the mustard.
2. Whisk briskly for a minute—work from the center out until it's smooth and glossy; no streaks of mustard left—scrape the sides with a spatula if it sticks; it'll look thick but pourable.
3. Taste—too sweet? More vinegar. Too tangy? More maple. Whisk again after tweaking—check the texture; too thick? A teaspoon of water. Too thin? More mustard.

4. Spoon into a jar with a tight lid—get every drop with your spatula. Let it sit at room temp for 10 minutes to settle—the flavors meld fast.
5. Refrigerate—it's good for a month. Stir before drizzling; use cold or warm.

**Nutritional Facts (per 1 tbsp / 15 ml):**

- Calories: 35
- Fat: 0 g
- Carbs: 8 g (Sugars: 7 g)
- Protein: 0 g
- Sodium: 200 mg

# Chapter 8: Mix & Match

Cooking's a bit like jazz—sometimes the best notes come when you riff off what's already there. I stumbled onto spicy mayo one lazy Sunday in Austin, staring at a fridge full of jars and a plate of leftover fries. I'd made some sriracha the week before, and there was a batch of classic mayo begging for a kick. A dollop of each, a quick stir, and suddenly those fries were singing a whole new tune—creamy, fiery, and gone in minutes. That's what this chapter's about: taking the sauces you've mastered and mixing 'em into something fresh. Here are ten combos to spark your own riffs—play around, tweak 'em, make 'em yours.

## 1. Spicy Mayo (Sriracha + Mayonnaise)

**Yield:** 1 cup (240 ml)

**Prep Time:** 10 minutes

**Ingredients:**

- ¾ cup (180 g) Classic Mayonnaise (Chapter 1)
- ¼ cup (60 ml) Sriracha (Chapter 2)
- 1 tsp (5 ml) lime juice

**Instructions:**

1. Scoop the classic mayonnaise into a medium bowl—use a spatula to get it all; it's the creamy backbone here. Measure the sriracha—eyeball it if you're brave—and pour it in with the lime juice for a little zing.
2. Grab a whisk—stir gently at first to mix the red into the white, then whisk briskly for 30 seconds; work from the center out until it's a smooth, peachy-orange blend—scrape the sides with your spatula to keep it even; no streaks left.
3. Check the texture—it should be thick and spoonable, clinging to the whisk. Too stiff? Add a teaspoon of water and whisk again. Too runny? More mayo—blend until it's just right.
4. Taste—too mild? Another squirt of sriracha. Too hot? More mayo to tame it. Whisk after each tweak—spoon into a jar with a tight lid; get every bit with your spatula.
5. Chill for 20 minutes in the fridge—the heat mellows into the creaminess. Stir before serving; keeps for a week.

**Nutritional Facts (per 1 tbsp / 15 ml):**

- Calories: 80
- Fat: 8 g (Saturated: 1 g)
- Carbs: 1 g (Sugars: 0 g)
- Protein: 0 g
- Sodium: 150 mg

## 2. BBQ Ranch (Barbecue Sauce + Ranch Dressing)

**Yield:** 1.5 cups (360 ml)

**Prep Time:** 10 minutes

**Ingredients:**

- 1 cup (240 ml) Smoky Barbecue Sauce (Chapter 1)
- ½ cup (120 g) Classic Ranch Dressing (Chapter 4)
- 1 tsp (5 g) smoked paprika

**Instructions:**

1. Pour the smoky barbecue sauce into a medium bowl—scrape the jar clean; it's the smoky star. Add the classic ranch dressing—spoon it in carefully—and sprinkle the smoked paprika over the top for extra depth.
2. Stir with a whisk—start slow to blend the thick barbecue with the creamy ranch, then whisk steadily for a minute; work it until it's a smooth, tan mix—scrape the sides with a spatula; no clumps or streaks.
3. Check the consistency—it should be creamy but pourable, coating the whisk lightly. Too thick? Add a tablespoon of water or milk and whisk again. Too thin? More ranch—mix until it feels right.
4. Taste—too tangy? A pinch of sugar. Too mild? More paprika or a dash of barbecue sauce. Whisk after adjusting—spoon into a jar with a lid; get it all in there.
5. Chill for 30 minutes in the fridge—the flavors marry up nicely. Stir before serving; keeps for a week.

**Nutritional Facts (per 2 tbsp / 30 ml):**

- Calories: 70
- Fat: 5 g (Saturated: 1 g)
- Carbs: 6 g (Sugars: 5 g)
- Protein: 1 g
- Sodium: 250 mg

### 3. Mustard-Chutney Glaze (Dijon Mustard + Spiced Apple Chutney)

**Yield:** 1 cup (240 ml)

**Prep Time:** 15 minutes

**Ingredients:**

- ½ cup (120 g) Dijon Mustard (Chapter 1)
- ½ cup (120 ml) Spiced Apple Chutney (Chapter 3)
- 1 tbsp (15 ml) honey

**Instructions:**

1. Measure the Dijon mustard into a medium bowl—scoop it smooth; it's the sharp base. Add the spiced apple chutney—spoon it in with its chunky bits—and drizzle the honey over the top for sweetness.
2. Stir with a wooden spoon—mix gently at first to blend the mustard's bite with the chutney's spice, then stir harder for a minute; work it until it's a cohesive, speckled glaze—scrape the sides with your spoon; keep the chunks intact.
3. Check the texture—it should be thick and spreadable, sticking to the spoon. Too stiff? Add a teaspoon of water and stir again. Too loose? More mustard—blend until it holds together.
4. Taste—too sharp? More honey. Too sweet? A dab of mustard. Stir after tweaking—spoon into a jar with a tight lid; scrape it clean with a spatula.

5. Let it sit at room temp for 15 minutes—the flavors settle fast. Refrigerate; keeps for a month—stir before glazing.

**Nutritional Facts (per 1 tbsp / 15 ml):**

- Calories: 35
- Fat: 0.5 g (Saturated: 0 g)
- Carbs: 7 g (Sugars: 5 g)
- Protein: 1 g
- Sodium: 150 mg

## 4. Harissa Aioli (Harissa + Garlic Aioli)

**Yield:** 1 cup (240 ml)

**Prep Time:** 10 minutes

**Ingredients:**

- ¾ cup (180 g) Garlic Aioli (Chapter 1)
- ¼ cup (60 ml) Harissa (Chapter 6)
- 1 tsp (5 ml) lemon juice

**Instructions:**

1. Scoop the garlic aioli into a medium bowl—use a spatula; it's rich and thick. Measure the harissa—spoon it carefully; it's spicy—and add it with the lemon juice for a bright lift.
2. Whisk gently at first—mix the red harissa into the creamy aioli, then whisk briskly for 30 seconds; blend until it's a smooth, coral-colored sauce—scrape the sides with your spatula; no streaks left.
3. Check the consistency—it should be creamy and spoonable, clinging to the whisk. Too thick? Add a teaspoon of water and whisk again. Too thin? More aioli—mix until it's just right.
4. Taste—too hot? More aioli. Too mild? Extra harissa. Whisk after each tweak—spoon into a jar with a lid; get every bit in there.
5. Chill for 20 minutes in the fridge—the heat balances with the garlic. Stir before serving; keeps for a week.

**Nutritional Facts (per 1 tbsp / 15 ml):**

- Calories: 90
- Fat: 9 g (Saturated: 1.5 g)
- Carbs: 1 g (Sugars: 0 g)
- Protein: 0 g
- Sodium: 120 mg

### 5. Chipotle Ranch (Chipotle Adobo Sauce + Ranch Dressing)
**Yield:** 1.5 cups (360 ml)

**Prep Time:** 10 minutes

**Ingredients:**

- 1 cup (240 g) Classic Ranch Dressing (Chapter 4)
- ¼ cup (60 ml) Chipotle Adobo Sauce (Chapter 6)
- 1 tbsp (15 ml) lime juice

**Instructions:**

1. Spoon the classic ranch dressing into a medium bowl—get it all; it's the creamy base. Add the chipotle adobo sauce—scoop it with its smoky kick—and pour in the lime juice for a tangy edge.
2. Stir with a whisk—start slow to blend the smoky red into the white, then whisk steadily for a minute; work it until it's a smooth, pinkish-tan mix—scrape the sides with your spatula; no clumps or streaks.
3. Check the texture—it should be thick but pourable, coating the whisk lightly. Too stiff? Add a teaspoon of milk and whisk again. Too runny? More ranch—blend until it feels right.
4. Taste—too spicy? More ranch. Too tame? Extra chipotle. Whisk after adjusting—spoon into a jar with a tight lid; scrape it clean.
5. Chill for 30 minutes in the fridge—the smokiness melds with the herbs. Stir before serving; keeps for a week.

**Nutritional Facts (per 2 tbsp / 30 ml):**

- Calories: 80
- Fat: 7 g (Saturated: 1 g)
- Carbs: 2 g (Sugars: 1 g)
- Protein: 1 g
- Sodium: 200 mg

## 6. Sweet Chili Mayo (Sweet Chili Sauce + Mayonnaise)
**Yield:** 1 cup (240 ml)

**Prep Time:** 10 minutes

**Ingredients:**

- ¾ cup (180 g) Classic Mayonnaise (Chapter 1)
- ¼ cup (60 ml) Sweet Chili Sauce (Chapter 3)
- 1 tsp (5 ml) rice vinegar

**Instructions:**

1. Scoop the classic mayonnaise into a medium bowl—use a spatula; it's the creamy foundation. Add the sweet chili sauce—spoon it with its sticky heat—and pour in the rice vinegar for a subtle tang.
2. Whisk gently at first—mix the red chili into the white mayo, then whisk briskly for 30 seconds; blend until it's a smooth, pale orange sauce—scrape the sides with your spatula; no streaks or clumps.
3. Check the consistency—it should be thick and spoonable, holding to the whisk. Too thick? Add a teaspoon of water and whisk again. Too thin? More mayo—mix until it's perfect.
4. Taste—too sweet? More vinegar. Too mild? Extra chili sauce. Whisk after tweaking—spoon into a jar with a lid; get every drop.
5. Chill for 20 minutes in the fridge—the sweet-spicy balance settles. Stir before serving; keeps for a week.

**Nutritional Facts (per 1 tbsp / 15 ml):**

- Calories: 85
- Fat: 8 g (Saturated: 1 g)
- Carbs: 3 g (Sugars: 2 g)
- Protein: 0 g
- Sodium: 120 mg

## 7. Gochujang BBQ (Gochujang + Smoky Barbecue Sauce)
**Yield:** 1.5 cups (360 ml)

**Prep Time:** 15 minutes

**Cook Time:** 10 minutes

**Ingredients:**

- 1 cup (240 ml) Smoky Barbecue Sauce (Chapter 1)
- ½ cup (120 g) Gochujang (Chapter 6)
- 1 tbsp (15 ml) sesame oil

**Instructions:**

1. Pour the smoky barbecue sauce into a small saucepan—scrape the jar; it's the smoky base. Add the gochujang—spoon it in with its fiery funk—and drizzle the sesame oil over the top for nuttiness.
2. Set over medium-low heat—stir with a wooden spoon for 2-3 minutes until the gochujang starts to melt into the barbecue sauce; keep going until it's a smooth, deep red mix—scrape the sides; it's thick.
3. Simmer for 5-7 minutes—stir every minute; it'll bubble gently and thicken a bit—don't let it burn; low heat's key. Taste—too spicy? More barbecue sauce. Too tame? Extra gochujang—stir after adjusting.
4. Cool in the pan for 10 minutes—stir occasionally; it'll firm up as it sits. Spoon into a jar with a funnel—get it all; it's sticky—then seal with a lid.

5. Refrigerate—it's good for a month. Warm gently before using; stir well.

**Nutritional Facts (per 2 tbsp / 30 ml):**

- Calories: 60
- Fat: 1 g (Saturated: 0 g)
- Carbs: 12 g (Sugars: 9 g)
- Protein: 1 g
- Sodium: 350 mg

## 8. Tzatziki Ranch (Tzatziki + Ranch Dressing)

**Yield:** 1.5 cups (360 ml)

**Prep Time:** 10 minutes

### Ingredients:

- 1 cup (240 g) Tzatziki (Chapter 2)
- ½ cup (120 g) Classic Ranch Dressing (Chapter 4)
- 1 tsp (5 g) chopped fresh dill

### Instructions:

1. Spoon the tzatziki into a medium bowl—get the cucumber bits too; it's the cool base. Add the classic ranch dressing—scoop it smooth—and rinse, pat dry, and chop the dill fine; sprinkle it in.
2. Stir with a whisk—start slow to blend the creamy ranch with the chunky tzatziki, then whisk steadily for a minute; work it until it's a smooth, green-flecked mix—scrape the sides with your spatula; keep the texture.
3. Check the consistency—it should be thick but pourable, coating the whisk. Too stiff? Add a teaspoon of milk and whisk again. Too runny? More tzatziki—blend until it's just right.
4. Taste—too mild? More dill. Too tangy? More ranch. Whisk after tweaking—spoon into a jar with a lid; scrape it clean.
5. Chill for 30 minutes in the fridge—the flavors deepen. Stir before serving; keeps for 5 days.

**Nutritional Facts (per 2 tbsp / 30 ml):**

- Calories: 50
- Fat: 4 g (Saturated: 1 g)
- Carbs: 2 g (Sugars: 1 g)
- Protein: 2 g
- Sodium: 150 mg

### 9. Peri-Peri Mayo (Peri-Peri Sauce + Mayonnaise)

**Yield:** 1 cup (240 ml)

**Prep Time:** 10 minutes

**Ingredients:**

- ¾ cup (180 g) Classic Mayonnaise (Chapter 1)
- ¼ cup (60 ml) Peri-Peri Sauce (Chapter 6)
- 1 tsp (5 ml) lemon juice

**Instructions:**

1. Scoop the classic mayonnaise into a medium bowl—use a spatula; it's the creamy star. Add the peri-peri sauce—spoon it with its fiery kick—and pour in the lemon juice for a bright twist.
2. Whisk gently at first—mix the red peri-peri into the white mayo, then whisk briskly for 30 seconds; blend until it's a smooth, orange-tinged sauce—scrape the sides with your spatula; no streaks left.
3. Check the texture—it should be thick and spoonable, clinging to the whisk. Too thick? Add a teaspoon of water and whisk again. Too thin? More mayo—mix until it's perfect.
4. Taste—too hot? More mayo. Too mild? Extra peri-peri. Whisk after adjusting—spoon into a jar with a tight lid; get every bit.
5. Chill for 20 minutes in the fridge—the heat balances with the cream. Stir before serving; keeps for a week.

**Nutritional Facts (per 1 tbsp / 15 ml):**

- Calories: 85
- Fat: 9 g (Saturated: 1 g)
- Carbs: 1 g (Sugars: 0 g)
- Protein: 0 g
- Sodium: 130 mg

## 10. Honey Mustard BBQ (Honey Mustard + Smoky Barbecue Sauce)

**Yield:** 1.5 cups (360 ml)

**Prep Time:** 15 minutes

**Ingredients:**

- ¾ cup (180 ml) Honey Mustard (Chapter 3)
- ¾ cup (180 ml) Smoky Barbecue Sauce (Chapter 1)
- 1 tbsp (15 ml) apple cider vinegar

**Instructions:**

1. Measure the honey mustard into a medium bowl—scoop it smooth; it's the sweet-tangy base. Pour in the smoky barbecue sauce—get it all; it's the smoky half—and add the apple cider vinegar for a sharp lift.
2. Stir with a wooden spoon—mix gently at first to blend the mustard's zing with the barbecue's smoke, then stir harder for a minute; work it until it's a smooth, golden-brown sauce—scrape the sides with your spoon; no separation.
3. Check the consistency—it should be thick and spreadable, sticking to the spoon. Too stiff? Add a teaspoon of water and stir again. Too loose? More barbecue sauce—blend until it holds together.
4. Taste—too sweet? More vinegar. Too mild? Extra barbecue sauce. Stir after tweaking—spoon into a jar with a lid; scrape it clean with a spatula.
5. Let it sit at room temp for 15 minutes—the flavors meld quick. Refrigerate; keeps for a month—stir before using.

**Nutritional Facts (per 2 tbsp / 30 ml):**

- Calories: 60
- Fat: 2 g (Saturated: 0 g)
- Carbs: 10 g (Sugars: 9 g)
- Protein: 0 g
- Sodium: 200 mg

# Appendix

Making sauces and condiments is a hands-on craft, and like any good adventure, it comes with a few bumps along the way. I've burned a batch or two in my time—Grandma Eula would've had a laugh—so I've put together this appendix to help you through the rough spots. Whether your mayo's splitting, your chutney's too salty, or you're missing a key ingredient, I've got you covered. Plus, there's a handy conversion chart and some tips on tracking down those hard-to-find goodies. Let's keep the kitchen fun and the flavors flowing.

### Troubleshooting Common Sauce-Making Issues

Sometimes things go sideways—here's how to fix 'em:

- **Emulsions Breaking (e.g., Mayonnaise, Aioli):** If your mayo looks curdled or oily, don't toss it. Start with a new bowl, add a fresh egg yolk and a teaspoon (5 ml) of water, and whisk. Slowly drizzle the broken batch into this, whisking constantly—go drop by drop at first, then a thin stream. It'll come back together with patience—keep the faith!
- **Sauce Too Salty:** Overdid the salt? Stir in a peeled, raw potato chunk and simmer for 10-15 minutes—it'll soak up some sodium. Remove it before finishing, then taste—add a splash of water or cream if it's still too much.
- **Too Thick (e.g., Gravy, BBQ Sauce):** If it's more paste than sauce, thin it out. Add a tablespoon (15 ml) of water, broth, or vinegar—depending on the recipe—and stir over low heat. Keep adding, a little at a time, until it's pourable but still rich.
- **Too Thin (e.g., Alfredo, Chutney):** If it's runny, simmer longer—5-10 minutes on low, stirring often—to reduce it. Or, whisk in a slurry (1 tsp / 5 g cornstarch + 1 tbsp / 15 ml water) and cook for 2-3 minutes until it thickens—don't overdo it; it sets more as it cools.
- **Burnt Bottom (e.g., Barbecue Sauce):** Caught it too late and it's scorched? Don't stir—pour the good stuff off the top into a new pot, leaving the burnt bits behind. Taste—if it's smoky but not bitter, you're golden; add a splash of vinegar to balance.
- **Fermentation Gone Funky (e.g., Sauerkraut, Hot Sauce):** If it smells off (rotten, not tangy) or has mold

beyond a skim-able layer, pitch it—safety first. Next time, ensure everything's submerged in brine, use clean tools, and check daily—white scum's okay, but green or black isn't.

- **Grainy Texture (e.g., Cheese Sauce):** If it's gritty, it's overheated. Whisk off the heat with a splash (1 tbsp / 15 ml) of cold milk or cream—keep going for a minute; strain through a fine sieve if it won't smooth out.
- **Too Spicy (e.g., Hot Sauce, Harissa):** Dial it back—stir in a tablespoon (15 g) of sugar, honey, or a creamy base like yogurt or mayo, depending on the vibe. Taste and repeat until it's tamed but still kicks.
- **Lacking Flavor:** Bland batch? Build it up—add a pinch of salt, a squeeze of citrus, or a dash of your base spice (e.g., smoked paprika for BBQ). Taste after each addition—small steps wake it up without overdoing it.
- **Separated Oil (e.g., Chili Oil):** If it's split, warm it gently over low heat and whisk hard for 30 seconds—it'll recombine. Cool and store properly—give it a shake before using next time.

## Substitution Guide for Dietary Needs

Running low or tweaking for diet? Here's what works:

- **Vegan:**
  - **Eggs (in Mayo, Aioli):** Swap with 3 tbsp (45 ml) aquafaba (chickpea liquid) per yolk—whisk it like crazy with oil for emulsion.
  - **Butter (e.g., Alfredo):** Use vegan butter or coconut oil—same amount; adjust salt since vegan butter varies.
  - **Cream (e.g., Alfredo):** Sub with full-fat coconut milk or cashew cream (blend ½ cup / 75 g cashews + ½ cup / 120 ml water)—match volume.
  - **Cheese (e.g., Cheddar Sauce):** Nutritional yeast (2 tbsp / 10 g per ½ cup / 60 g cheese) or vegan cheese shreds—melt carefully.
- **Gluten-Free:**
  - **Flour (e.g., Gravy):** Use cornstarch (1 tbsp / 8 g per 2 tbsp / 16 g flour) or gluten-free all-purpose flour—whisk into a slurry first.
  - **Soy Sauce (e.g., Worcestershire):** Tamari or coconut aminos—same amount; tamari's saltier, so taste as you go.
- **Low-Sodium:**
  - **Salt:** Cut by half and boost with herbs (1 tsp / 2 g per tsp salt) or lemon zest—add gradually; taste often.
  - **Soy Sauce:** Low-sodium soy or dilute regular with water (1:1)—adjust other flavors up to compensate.
- **Sugar-Free:**

- - **Sugar (e.g., Ketchup, BBQ):** Use erythritol or stevia (1 tsp / 4 g per ¼ cup / 50 g sugar)—start small; they're sweeter gram-for-gram.
  - **Honey (e.g., Honey Mustard):** Sugar-free honey substitute or mashed dates (2 tbsp / 30 g per ¼ cup / 60 ml)—blend smooth.
- **Nut-Free:**
  - **Peanut Butter (e.g., Thai Peanut Sauce):** Sunflower seed butter—same amount; it's less sweet, so tweak sugar if needed.
  - **Tahini:** Seedless version or blended silken tofu (½ cup / 120 g per ½ cup / 120 g tahini)—adjust water for texture.
- **Dairy-Free:**
  - **Sour Cream (e.g., Ranch):** Coconut yogurt or blended silken tofu (same amount)—add a splash of lemon for tang.
  - **Buttermilk:** Mix 1 cup (240 ml) plant milk + 1 tbsp (15 ml) vinegar—let sit 5 minutes before using.

## Measurement Conversion Chart

No guesswork—here's the math done for you:

- **Volume:**
  - 1 tsp = 5 ml
  - 1 tbsp = 15 ml (3 tsp)
  - ¼ cup = 60 ml (4 tbsp)
  - ⅓ cup = 80 ml (5 tbsp + 1 tsp)
  - ½ cup = 120 ml (8 tbsp)
  - ¾ cup = 180 ml (12 tbsp)
  - 1 cup = 240 ml (16 tbsp)
  - 1 pint = 480 ml (2 cups)
  - 1 quart = 960 ml (4 cups)
- **Weight:**
  - 1 oz = 28 g
  - 2 oz = 56 g
  - 4 oz = 113 g (¼ lb)
  - 8 oz = 225 g (½ lb)
  - 16 oz = 450 g (1 lb)
  - 32 oz = 900 g (2 lb)
- **Common Ingredients (Approximate):**
  - Flour: 1 cup = 120 g
  - Sugar: 1 cup = 200 g
  - Brown Sugar (packed): 1 cup = 220 g
  - Butter: 1 cup = 225 g (2 sticks)
  - Honey: 1 cup = 340 g
  - Salt: 1 tsp = 6 g
- **Temperature:**
  - 300°F = 150°C
  - 350°F = 175°C
  - 400°F = 200°C

- 450°F = 230°C

**Resources for Sourcing Unique Ingredients**

Finding the good stuff can be a hunt—here's where to look:

- **Spices (e.g., Gochugaru, Smoked Paprika, Szechuan Peppercorns):**
  - **Local:** Hit up spice shops or international markets—Korean or Middle Eastern stores often stock gochugaru; Latin markets have smoked paprika.
  - **Online:** Penzeys Spices (penzeys.com), The Spice House (thespicehouse.com), or Amazon—search for bulk options; check reviews for freshness.
- **Dried Chilies (e.g., Chipotle, Scotch Bonnet, Bird's Eye):**
  - **Local:** Mexican or Caribbean grocery stores—look in the dried goods aisle; they're cheap and potent.
  - **Online:** MexGrocer (mexgrocer.com) or Chili Pepper Madness (shop.chilipeppermadness.com)—ships fresh; store in airtight jars.
- **Fermentation Supplies (e.g., Sea Salt, Jars, Weights):**
  - **Local:** Health food stores for non-iodized sea salt; hardware stores or kitchen shops for mason jars and weights.
  - **Online:** Cultures for Health (culturesforhealth.com)—kits and gear; Amazon for jars (search "wide-mouth quart").
- **Specialty Items (e.g., Tamarind Paste, Fish Sauce, Truffle Oil):**

- **Local:** Asian markets for tamarind and fish sauce—check the condiment aisle; gourmet stores for truffle oil.
- **Online:** iHerb (iherb.com) or Thrive Market (thrivemarket.com)—wide selection; look for deals on small batches.
- **Fresh Herbs and Produce (e.g., Ginger, Dill, Mangoes):**
  - **Local:** Farmers' markets for peak freshness—ask vendors for bulk herbs; ethnic grocers for ginger and mangoes year-round.
  - **Online:** Misfits Market (misfitsmarket.com)—delivers oddball produce cheap; great for experimenting.
- **Tips:**
  - Call ahead to local spots—stock varies. Online, buy small first to test quality—store spices in cool, dark places; freeze extra chilies or herbs in zip-tops to stretch 'em.

Printed in Dunstable, United Kingdom

78224483R00107